T0323089

CAMPAIGN 349

WARSAW 1920

The War for the Eastern Borderlands

STEVEN J. ZALOGA

ILLUSTRATED BY STEVE NOON

Series editor Marcus Cowper

OSPREY PUBLISHING
Bloomsbury Publishing Plc

Kemp House, Chawley Park, Cumnor Hill, Oxford OX2 9PH, UK
29 Earlsfort Terrace, Dublin 2, Ireland
1385 Broadway, 5th Floor, New York, NY 10018, USA
Email: info@ospreypublishing.com
www.ospreypublishing.com

OSPREY is a trademark of Osprey Publishing Ltd

First published in Great Britain in 2020
Transferred to digital print in 2024

A catalogue record for this book is available from the British Library.

Print ISBN: 978 1 4728 3729 5
ePub: 978 1 4728 3730 1
ePDF: 978 1 4728 3728 8
XML: 978 1 4728 3727 1

Maps by www.bounford.com
3D BEVs by The Black Spot
Index by Nick Hayhurst
Typeset by PDQ Digital Media Solutions, Bungay, UK
Printed and bound in India by Replika Press Private Ltd.

24 25 26 27 28   10 9 8 7 6 5 4 3

Artist's note

Readers may care to note that the original paintings from which the colour
plates in this book were prepared are available for private sale. All
reproduction copyright whatsoever is retained by the publishers. The artist
can be contacted via the following website:

https://www.steve-noon.co.uk

The publishers regret that they can enter into no correspondence upon
this matter.

Osprey Publishing supports the Woodland Trust, the UK's leading woodland
conservation charity.

To find out more about our authors and books visit
www.ospreypublishing.com. Here you will find extracts, author
interviews, details of forthcoming events and the option to sign up for
our newsletter.

Author's note

Geography in the Borderlands presents an intractable and contentious
problem, since most locations have different spellings in the different
languages – for example, Lwów (Polish), Lvov (Russian), Lviv (Ukrainian) and
Lemberg (German). I have used English names for well-known locations
(e.g. Warsaw rather than Warszawa, Vistula rather than Wisła). For other
locations, I have generally used the place names in effect after the 1921
Treaty of Riga, though for important locations, I have identified them by
other major identities on first use.

Unless otherwise indicated, the photographs that appear in this work are
from the author's collection.

Acronyms and abbreviations

BS	*Biuro Szyfrów*: Cypher Office
DA-UNR	*Dieva Armiya*: Regular Army of the UNR
PPS	*Polska Partia Socjalistyczna*: Polish Socialist Party
RKKA	*Raboche Krestyanskaya Krasnaya Armiya*: Workers' and Peasants' Red Army
RVSR	*Revolyutsionny Voyenny Soviet Respubliki*: Revolutionary Military Council of the Republics
UHA	*Ukrayinska Halytska Armiya*: Ukrainian Galician Army (of the ZUNR)
UNR	*Ukrainskaya Narodnaya Respublika*: Ukrainian People's Republic
VCheKa	*Vserossiyskaya chrezvychaynaya komissiya po borbe s kontrrevolyutsiyey i sabotazhem*: All-Russian Emergency Commission for Combatting Counter-Revolution and Sabotage
VOKR	*Voenizirovannaya Okhrana*: Armed Guards
VSYuR	*Vooruzhyonniye sily Yuga Rossii*, Armed Forces of South Russia
ZUNR	*Zakhidno Ukrayinska Narodna Respublika*: Western Ukrainian People's Republic

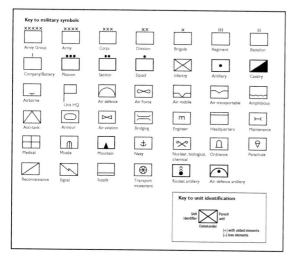

PREVIOUS PAGE
The Polish 22nd Siedlice Infantry Regiment on the march in the
summer of 1920.

CONTENTS

ORIGINS OF THE CAMPAIGN

The Battle of Warsaw in August 1920 has been called the Eighteenth Decisive Battle of the World.[1] The Red Army appeared to be on the verge of advancing through Poland into Germany to expand the Bolshevik revolution. Had the war spread into Germany, the Great War would have reignited, dragging in France and Britain. In the event, the Red Army was defeated by 'the miracle on the Vistula'.

This book examines the roots and outcomes of this conflict in Europe's Eastern Borderlands. Following the collapse of the three European empires – Germany, Austro-Hungary and Russia – an independent Poland re-emerged from the partitions of the late 18th century. The boundaries of Poland and the other resurrected central European nations were not defined and were settled on the battlefield.

The tactics of the Russo-Polish War of 1919–21 stood in considerable contrast to the trench fighting of the Great War. The low density of forces on both sides as well as the enormous distances made this a war of manoeuvre. The conflict saw a curious mixture of traditional and advanced tactics and technology. Horse cavalry played a crucial role in the fighting, but airplanes, tanks, armoured trains and radios gave the war a thin veneer of modernity.

1   Lord Edgar Vincent D'Abernon, *The Eighteenth Decisive Battle of the World: Warsaw, 1920*, Hodder & Stoughton, London: 1920.

The Bolshevik revolution in November 1917 ignited a series of conflicts around the periphery of the Russian empire. This is a Red Army unit on parade in Red Square in Moscow in February 1919 with the State Historical Museum on the north side of the square in the background.

The strategic situation, November 1918–January 1920

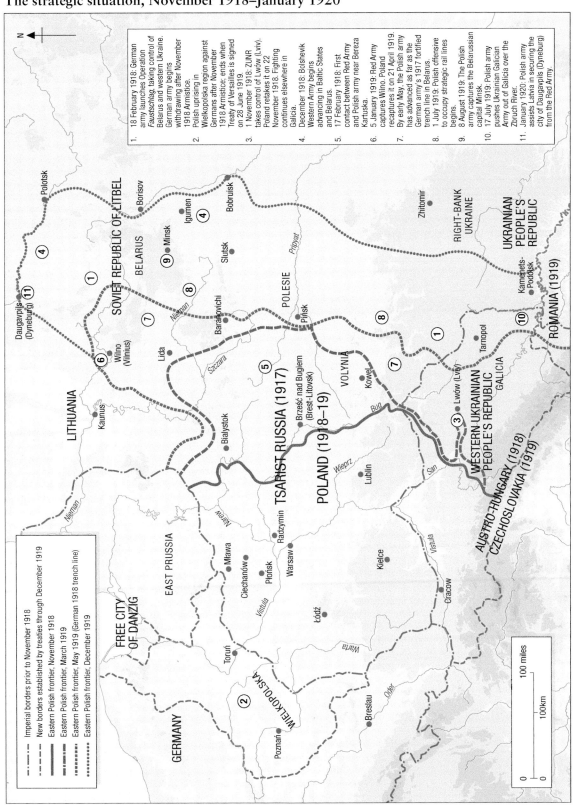

1. 18 February 1918: German army launches Operation *Faustschlag*, taking control of Belarus and western Ukraine. German army begins withdrawing after November 1918 Armistice.

2. Polish uprising in Wielkopolska region against Germans after November 1918 Armistice; ends when Treaty of Versailles is signed on 28 June 1919.

3. 1 November 1918: ZUNR takes control of Lwów (Lviv). Poland retakes it on 22 November 1918. Fighting continues elsewhere in Galicia.

4. December 1918: Bolshevik Western Army begins advancing in Baltic States and Belarus.

5. 17 February 1918: First contact between Red Army and Polish army near Bereza Kartuska.

6. 5 January 1919: Red Army captures Wilno. Poland recaptures it on 21 April 1919. By early May, the Polish army has advanced as far as the German army's 1917 fortified trench line in Belarus.

7. 1 July 1919: Polish offensive to occupy strategic rail lines begins.

8. 8 August 1919: The Polish army captures the Belarussian capital Minsk.

9. 17 July 1919: Polish army pushes Ukrainian Galician Army out of Galicia over the Zbruch River.

10. January 1920: Polish army assists Latvia in securing the city of Daugavpils (Dyneburg) from the Red Army.

Imperial borders prior to November 1918
New borders established by treaties through December 1919
Eastern Polish frontier, November 1918
Eastern Polish frontier, March 1919
Eastern Polish frontier, May 1919 (German 1918 trench line)
Eastern Polish frontier, December 1919

0   100 miles
0   100km

5

The issues at the heart of the war were never satisfactorily resolved and were a critical ingredient in the 1939–45 conflicts in the region.

THE STRATEGIC SITUATION

Poland ceased to exist as an independent state after the series of three partitions by the neighbouring empires between 1772 and 1795. Imperial Russia controlled the largest portion, called Congress Poland, which included Warsaw. Prussia controlled the western provinces of Pomerania and Silesia, a region called Wielkopolska. Austro-Hungary controlled the south-east region of Galicia, including the old imperial capital of Kraków. Napoleon briefly recreated a rump Grand Duchy of Poland and there were substantial rebellions in Russian Poland in 1830–31 and 1863.

The rise of modern nationalism in the Polish lands in the late 19th century was met with varying imperial responses. Austro-Hungary attempted to mollify its rambunctious nationalities by allowing a degree of cultural autonomy so long as imperial rule was not directly challenged. As a result, there were vigorous national movements in the Polish and Ukrainian regions. Russia attempted to suppress Polish culture and to Russify the region, which bred further rebellion. Prussia, and later unified Germany, adopted anti-Catholic policies and attempted to Germanize the Wielkopolska region, once again intensifying Polish national sentiment.

Much of the fighting on the Eastern Front between 1914 and 1917 took place in the Polish provinces of Russia and Austro-Hungary, and about a million civilians died in this region during the war. The Russian army adopted a scorched-earth policy during its retreat, leaving desolation through the Borderlands. By 1919, about a third of the civilians in this region were on the brink of starvation and there were waves of influenza and typhus epidemics.

Poles had been drafted into all three imperial armies, and about 400,000 Polish soldiers died in the conflict. Polish leaders, most notably Józef Piłsudski, created semi-autonomous Polish military formations during the war years with the support of Austro-Hungary. Germany attempted to create

In early 1918 the German army staged Operation *Faustschlag*, forcing the Bolsheviks to sign the Treaty of Brest-Litovsk in March 1918. This put the control of the Borderlands in German hands for most of 1918. Here, a pair of German field guns engage a Bolshevik armoured train on the outskirts of Narva, Estonia, on 28 March 1918.

a Polish vassal state, the Regency Council, in 1917, in the hope of reinforcing its struggle with Russia. This was widely rejected by the Poles and Piłsudski was thrown into jail for refusing to align his Polish units with Germany. This cemented his reputation as Poland's premier soldier and leader.

The Borderlands as battleground

The Borderlands refers to the region of contemporary Poland, Ukraine, Belarus and the Baltic States. From a military standpoint, operations have traditionally been shaped by its distinct geographic features. The Polesie region between Belarus and Ukraine includes the Pripyat marshlands, dividing the region, since these wetlands are poorly suited to military campaigns. As a result, there are two traditional warpaths through the Borderlands.

The northern warpath, sometimes called the Smolensk Gate, had been the traditional route between Poland and the Tsarist capital of Petrograd (St Petersburg) as well as the Soviet capital of Moscow. This was the route of Napoleon's invasion. The southern warpath passes through Polish/Ukrainian Galicia towards Kiev and the Black Sea. The 1919–20 Russo-Polish War was fought along both of these warpaths.

On 29 April 1918, General Pavel Skoropadsky staged a *coup d'état* in Kiev against the Ukrainian People's Republic with the connivance of the German army. He is seen here on the right, meeting with the German chief of the general staff, Field Marshal Paul von Hindenburg, on the left.

The demographic features of the region were a contributing factor of the wars of 1917–20. The Borderlands are one of Europe's ethnographic fault lines. The area is primarily Slavic but of various religions: Catholic in the Polish areas, and Uniate and Orthodox to the east. The area was also home to most of Europe's Jewish community. The Baltic States were ethnically and linguistically distinct. There was no neat division between these communities, which made the establishment of borders based along ethnic lines so difficult for the diplomats.

Most of the areas under Russian rule were undergoing an upsurge of nationalism. Lithuania and the other Baltic States rejected Russification and sought their own independent states. The Ukrainian provinces of Austro-Hungary and Russia presented a much more complex situation. Western Ukraine, especially Galicia, had a flourishing national movement under Austro-Hungarian rule. Right-Bank (of the Dnieper) Ukraine, the Tsarist provinces centred on Kiev, saw stirrings of an independent national identity. The industrialized areas of Left-Bank Ukraine, centred on Kharkov, were less inclined to Ukrainian separatism and were more comfortable in Russia's orbit. While Ukrainian nationalists dreamed of a unified and independent Ukraine encompassing all these regions, there remained substantial disharmony.

The one area with a very weak national movement was Belarus. Its major cities including Minsk had largely Jewish, Polish and Russian populations. Likewise, its gentry tended to be Polish or Russian. The Orthodox clergy in the rural areas were under the influence of the Russian Church. Belarus lacked a large urban Belarussian bourgeois and intelligentsia that was the usual basis for the nationalist movements of this period; the peasantry lacked strong national identity.

From a Polish perspective, the two most contentious areas were the cities of Wilno (Vilnius) on the Polish-Lithuanian/Belarussian frontier, and Lwów (Lviv) on the Polish-Ukrainian frontier in Galicia. Both these cities had been Polish outposts in the days of the Polish-Lithuanian Republic. In 1919, the majority of the population was Polish and Jewish. However, Lithuania viewed Vilnius as its natural capital, and likewise the Western Ukrainian region viewed Lviv as its national centre.

Turmoil in Ukraine

The Russian revolutions of February and November 1917 ignited the Russian civil wars that inevitably spilled over into the Borderlands. When Lenin's Bolshevik coup in Petrograd in November 1917 overthrew the short-lived Provisional Government, it created a power vacuum in the outlying regions of Russia. Ukrainian nationalists in Kiev declared the formation of the Ukrainian People's Republic (*Ukrainskaya Narodnaya Respublika* – UNR) on 20 November 1917, along with the creation of a Ukrainian army. In late December 1917, Bolshevik forces responded by creating a rival government in Kharkov and moving Red Guard units into Ukraine, capturing Kiev on 8–9 February 1918. Control of Kiev would change 11 times during the years of civil war.

After peace talks between Russia and the Central Powers stalled, Berlin used the turmoil as the excuse for Operation *Faustschlag* (*Fist Punch*). This 11-day campaign routed the Bolshevik army and put Germany in control of most of the Borderlands from the Baltic States in the north through to Ukraine on the Black Sea. In the face of this military calamity, Lenin's Bolshevik government acquiesced to the Treaty of Brest-Litovsk on 3 March 1918 that ceded control of Ukraine and Belarus to the Central Powers.

The German army at first recognized the Ukrainian government, but concern over the chaotic conditions in the country led Field Marshal Hermann von Eichhorn to gradually take over administrative control. On 26 and 27 April, the nascent Ukrainian army was disarmed. With German connivance, General Pavel Skoropadsky staged a coup two days later and declared himself *Hetman* (warlord) of Ukraine. The Germans permitted the formation of a modest number of Ukrainian military units during the reign of Skoropadsky's Hetmanate.

The defeat of the Central Powers in November 1918 and the subsequent evacuation of the German army triggered a new series of conflicts over who would control the Borderlands. In Ukraine, Simon Petliura's Directorate staged a coup against Skoropadsky and put the UNR government back in control in Kiev. A new Ukrainian army, the *Dieva Armiya* (DA-UNR), was formed from the remnants of the Hetmanate army as well as new formations.

By early 1919, the DA-UNR was fighting on four fronts. The Left-Bank (of the Dnieper) Group was fighting against the Bolsheviks and the anti-Bolshevik White Russian armies. The Northern/Right-Bank Group was fighting against the Bolsheviks and the Poles. The Southern Group was fighting against the French and Greek intervention forces around Odessa. The Dniester Group was fighting against Romania in the contested area south-west of Odessa.

The Ukrainian capital of Kiev changed hands 11 times between 1917 and 1920. This is Ataman Andrei Shkuro, who led the Cossack Cavalry Corps in Denikin's Volunteer Army shortly before their capture of Kiev from Petliura's forces in August 1919.

France intervened in Ukraine in mid-December 1918, sending troops to the port of Odessa in support of the anti-Bolshevik Armed Forces of South Russia (*Vooruzhyonniye sily Yuga Rossii*, VSYuR). This intervention was short-lived. In the face of troop munities, the French withdrew in March 1919 without any significant fighting. In the meantime, the Red Army overwhelmed the weak Ukrainian army and seized Kiev again on 5 February, pushing out Petliura's government. Bolshevik control of Ukraine was far from secure due to the weakness of its forces and the chaotic conditions in the countryside. In April and May 1919, there was a violent spasm of peasant revolts, triggered by draconian Bolshevik food requisitions and the brutality of the VCheKa police (*Vserossiyskaya chrezvychaynaya komissiya po borbe s kontrrevolyutsiyey i sabotazhem* – the All-Russian Emergency Commission for Combatting Counter-Revolution and Sabotage).

While the fighting in Right-Bank Ukraine had pitted Ukrainian forces against Bolshevik and White Russian armies, the conflict in Galician Ukraine pitted the West Ukrainian People's Republic (*Zakhidno Ukrayinska Narodna Respublika* – ZUNR) against Poland. The conflict ignited on 1 November 1918 when the ZUNR's militias took control of the contested city of Lwów. The Poles quickly rallied and retook most of the city by 22 November 1918, though fighting continued through the area as the ZUNR laid siege to Lwów and neighbouring Polish strongholds such as the fortress city of Przemyśl.

The ZUNR and Petliura's UNR nominally joined in a unified Ukraine on 22 January 1919. This was only a political gesture as both governments remained independent with their own armies and their own foreign policies. The ZUNR's military policy was strongly anti-Polish, while the focus of Petliura's UNR was against Bolshevik and White Russian attempts to reassert Russian control over Right-Bank Ukraine.

Poland was able to mobilize substantially greater forces than the ZUNR's Ukrainian Galician Army (*Ukrayinska Halytska Armiya* – UHA). By the end

A company from the Polish 85th Wilno Rifle Regiment on the march during the fighting for Slutsk in August 1919. During the fighting around Slutsk, this regiment served as part of Colonel Aleksander Boruszczak's 3rd Lithuanian-Belarussian Brigade.

of July 1919, the Polish army had pushed the remnants of the UHA east to the Zbruch River. From July to September 1919, both the ZUNR and UNR had their governments co-located at Kamenets-Podolsk, south of Kiev.

By March 1919, the Red Army had a combat strength of 308,500 bayonets and 24,500 sabres. Most of this was deployed in Ukraine against the Ukrainian forces and the White Russian forces, amounting to 192,000 bayonets and 21,000 sabres. The rest of the Red Army was fighting against small White Russian armies in Siberia, Crimea and the Caucasus.

Aid from the Entente to the Armed Forces of South Russia greatly increased the military power of the White Russian armies in the summer of 1919. As a result, in July 1919, General Anton Denikin's Volunteer Army began expanding outwards from the Black Sea coast towards Moscow and Kiev. When the Red Army evacuated Kiev in August 1919, the city was entered by both Petliura's Ukrainian army and Denikin's troops. The Volunteer Army was unwilling to support any separatist movement and ejected the Ukrainians from the city.

By the late summer of 1919, the two Ukrainian states had lost control of Ukraine except for a small enclave south of Zhitomir. On 1 September, the ZUNR reached an armistice with Poland. This ended the fighting in Galicia for the time being, and turned the focus of the Ukrainian military efforts against the Bolsheviks and White Russians. At the time, the allied Ukrainian armies had about 85,000 troops, with an effective combat strength of about 12,000 in the UHA and 20,000 in the DA-UNR. This was far smaller than any of their major opponents.

Further Ukrainian military action against Denikin's Volunteer Army largely collapsed in September and October 1919 due to an outbreak of typhus. In late 1919, the UHA had 29,770 troops but an effective strength of only 5,420 due to the typhus epidemic; it evaporated due to widespread desertions. The ZUNR government warned Petliura that they had to abandon the joint struggle, and they reached a truce with the Volunteer Army in November 1919. Petliura's UNR was forced to abandon its capital in Kamenets-Podolsk, shifting to Zhmerinka. By November 1919, the DA-UNR had been reduced to only about 3,000 troops. In December 1919, it was forced to abandon conventional military operations and resort to guerrilla warfare.

The advance of Denikin's Volunteer Army on Moscow was defeated by the Red Army in the late autumn of 1919. The White Russians retreated back towards Crimea in November and December 1919. The Red Army surged back into Ukraine again, taking control of Kiev once more on 16 December from Volunteer Army rearguards.

Turmoil in Belarus and the Baltics

The Bolshevik seizure of power in Petrograd in November 1917 had ripple effects down the Baltic coast. In November 1917, Estonia declared independence, though it was quickly

suppressed by the nearby Bolshevik forces from Petrograd. Likewise, the Bolsheviks invaded Latvia on 5 December 1918 after the declaration of the Republic of Latvia. The Kingdom of Lithuania was declared on 16 February 1918, but proved stillborn due to the presence of the German army.

During the defence of Lwów in 1919, the Women's Volunteer Legion (*Ochotnicza Legia Kobiet* – OLK) recruited young women to assist the Polish cause. In the background is the founder of the OLK, Lieutenant-Colonel Aleksandra Zagórska. During the August 1920 defence of Warsaw, a women's battalion took part in the fighting.

As in Ukraine, the German army launched Operation *Faustschlag* on 18 February 1918 to take control of the northern Borderlands from the Bolsheviks. With the defeat of the Central Powers in November 1918, the three Baltic republics attempted to re-assert their independence from Russia. These wars were complicated by the lingering presence of numerous German units in the region, which challenged the Baltic independence movements. In the summer of 1919, the western Entente of Britain and France insisted that the German troops be removed. Berlin pretended that they were local formations outside their control. In October 1919, Britain supported General Nikolai Yudenich's anti-Bolshevik Army of North-Western Russia that was operating from Estonia to capture Petrograd. The military campaigns in the Baltic area in this period were far too complex to detail in this short book.

In the wake of the November 1918 German capitulation, Lenin decided to begin military actions further to the west in the hope of encouraging a Marxist revolution in Germany. The operation was codenamed 'Target Vistula', since Poland stood in the way of a Red Army operation to Germany. The Western Army (or Front) was created on 15 November 1918 to carry out this mission. Its initial core was the Western Rifle Division, made up largely of Polish troops and intended to be the core of an eventual Soviet Polish army. The Western Front eventually grew to three divisions: the Pskov Division aimed at Wilno, the Western Rifle Division aimed at Grodno and Białystok, and the 17th Rifle Division aimed at Brest-Litovsk (Brześć-nad-Bugiem). This army was quite small, numbering only 19,000 troops at the end of 1919, but it was operating in an area virtually devoid of opposing forces since the German troops usually retreated on contact.

The city of Minsk was taken by the Bolsheviks on 11 December 1918. The Belarussian *Rada* (council) had been formed there in March 1918 but it had been unable to form a Belarussian army, since the area was under German occupation.

A shortage of weapons during the defence of Lwów led to some curious improvisations. This steam-punk tank named *Kresowiec* (Borderlander) was built by staff of the Lwów Polytechnic in April 1919 on the basis of a Praga or Stock tricycle steam tractor.

Poles in Wilno set up a self-defence force, and requested assistance from Warsaw. However, a substantial body of German troops continued to retreat through the area, and Berlin refused to permit Polish army passage. Piłsudski's government warned Petrograd that occupation of Wilno would be considered a *casus belli*, but the Western Army ignored this threat. When confronted by two Bolshevik rifle divisions, the two Polish regiments in Wilno withdrew. The city was occupied by the Bolsheviks on 5 January 1919.

The new head of the Red Army, Leon Trotsky, recommended against any further advance into Polish territory in view of the weakness of the Western Army. Instead, Lenin decided to shift a portion of the Northern Front from the defence of Petrograd to assist in the drive west. On 8 February 1919, the Red Army started an offensive over the Nieman River near Alitius to cut off the Lithuanian city of Kaunus from East Prussia. German forces intervened and defeated the Bolshevik force.

On 5 February 1919, Warsaw and Berlin signed an agreement to permit Polish troops to intervene against the Bolsheviks. An operational group under General Wacław Iwaszkiewicz headed east of Białystok while a second group under General Antoni Listowski headed into the area near Brest-Litovsk. Three other groups were deployed towards Ukraine at the same time, but faced Ukrainian rather than Bolshevik forces. The first fighting between the Poles and the Bolsheviks took place near Bereza Kartuska on 17 February 1919, when a Bolshevik detachment was defeated by Major Władysław Dąbrowski's cavalry regiment.

To avoid the appearance of having provoked the Russo-Polish conflict, Lenin decided to create a buffer zone of nominally independent Soviet puppet states. On 1 January 1919, the Bolsheviks announced the creation of a Belarussian Socialist Republic. This was short-lived and instead, on 28 February, the Soviet Republic of Lithuania and Belarus, called Litbel, was created in its place. Shortly after, the Western Army was re-designated as the Lithuanian-Belarussian Army. By this stage, it had risen in strength to 49,000 troops. However, its confrontations with German and Polish troops made clear that it lacked adequate leadership and training. In spite of its impressive new name, this army was a hollow force, suffering from poor discipline and often on the brink of famine. Two regiments of the Western Rifle Division mutinied, followed by regiments in Gomel.

Military operations in the area came to a halt in March and April 1919, largely due to the weather and muddy conditions. After unsuccessful peace talks, the Polish army attacked on 15 and 16 April. A group under General Józef Lasocki struck the main Bolshevik concentration near Lida. Another operational group under General Edward Śmigły-Rydz infiltrated around the north-western flank of the Bolshevik defence line and made a 100km dash for Wilno. After two days of fighting, Wilno was in Polish hands on 21 April 1919. By early May, the Poles had reached the German army's 1917 fortified trench line in Belarus.

A typhus epidemic broke out in the Borderlands in the autumn of 1919, largely destroying the Ukrainian army. An Interallied Medical Commission organized by the League of Red Cross Societies was sent to Poland in the hope of halting its spread to Western Europe and America. Here, the commission members are being taken on a tour of the POW camp at Brest-Litovsk by Major-General Józef Szamota on 28 October 1919 to see the extent of the contagion among Bolshevik and Ukrainian troops.

The performance of the Red Army against the Poles was so abysmal that on 2 June, Lenin, Trotsky and the senior Bolshevik leaders decided on a wholesale reorganization of the Western Front, removing the entire senior command of the Litbel army. Although it had been intended to be a model for revolutionary military units in the Borderlands, its poor performance led to the decision to reconfigure the force along conventional military lines.

There was a lull in the Russo-Polish fighting in late spring. Germany had not signed the Treaty of Versailles, which was supposed to establish Poland's western frontiers. As a result, the Polish army had to keep its Wielkopolska regiments in reserve for possible action against the Germans. The treaty was finally signed on 28 June 1919, allowing the Polish army to shift its forces to the east. Beyond the reinforcements from the German frontier, the Haller Army that had been raised in France finally arrived in Poland.

By late summer, the Red Army had been forced to turn its attention to other theatres. The summer and early autumn of 1919 were the high tide of the anti-Bolshevik White Russian armies. In May 1919, Yudenich's Army of North-Western Russia began its advances on Petrograd. Due to the city's proximity to foreign borders, Lenin had moved the capital from Petrograd to Moscow in March 1919. However, Petrograd was still one of Russia's main industrial centres and had to be defended at all costs. On 3 July 1919, Denikin's Volunteer Army began its march through Ukraine towards Moscow as previously described.

Under these circumstances, Piłsudski planned a broad offensive that was aimed at pushing the Polish frontier far enough east to control the strategic north–south railway line that ran from Polotsk in north-western Belarus to Równe in Ukraine. The offensive began on 1 July, and by 8 August, the Polish army had taken the Belarussian capital of Minsk. Once its objectives were secured, the Polish army took up defensive positions.

At the time, Piłsudski boasted that the Polish army could have gone all the way to Moscow in 1919. He refrained from doing so while the White Russian armies continued to advance on Petrograd and Moscow. The White Russian governments had made clear that in the event of their victory, they planned to reincorporate Poland back into a 'United Russia'. The Entente urged that the Poles intervene to assist the White Russian advance, whom

This is a typical example of the type of improvised armoured train widely used by all sides during the conflict in the Borderlands. This particular example, *Śmiały Szeroki* (*Bold-Wide*), was assembled in the Wilno railyards in May 1919. It had the 'Wide' suffix in its name to indicate that it operated on the wide Russian gauge (1,520mm) rather than the standard European gauge (1,435mm). It was armed with Russian 76mm M.02 field guns, and was used in support of the Polish 1st Legion Infantry Division in the Lithuania–Belarus region.

they were supporting. Rather than assist the White Russians, Piłsudski decided to let the Bolshevik and White Russian armies batter each other. Not only did Piłsudski refuse to support the White Russian advance, he informed Lenin through back channels that Poland would take no part in support of the White Russian campaign, encouraging him to shift Red Army forces away from the existing Polish–Soviet frontier to fight Denikin.

The Borderlands at the end of 1919

The year 1919 had started out in considerable chaos with several armies contesting the control of the Borderlands. By the end of 1919, the situation was much more clearly defined. The three Baltic States had gained control over their territories, even though some significant fighting would continue into 1920. The Polish army controlled much of the remainder of the western Borderlands from Belarus in the north through Volynia to eastern Galicia in the south. The Red Army controlled the eastern regions of Belarus as well as Right-Bank and Left-Bank Ukraine. The dying embers of the Ukrainian army were kept alive by promises of Polish aid.

Bolshevik Russia and Poland began peace negotiations in the autumn of 1919, but these were conducted in bad faith. Both sides expected further military actions in 1920, and were preparing their armies for a future confrontation over control of the Borderlands.

A Polish army unit marching near the Russian Orthodox cathedral on Saxon Place in Warsaw in May 1919.

CHRONOLOGY

1917

7 November	Bolshevik revolution in Petrograd.
20 November	Ukrainian National Republic founded in Kiev.

1918

15 January	Red Army is founded.
18 February	German army starts Operation *Faustschlag* in the Borderlands.
3 March	Brest-Litovsk Treaty signed between Bolsheviks and Germany.
9 March	Belarussian National Republic proclaimed in Minsk.
29 April	General Pavel Skoropadsky overthrows Ukrainian government, declares himself *Hetman*.
November	Western Ukrainian People's Republic declared in Lviv.
11 November	Germany calls for armistice; World War I ends. Polish Second Republic declared in Warsaw.
28 November	Poles take Lwów back from Ukrainian Galician Army.

1919

5 January	Wilno taken from Poles by Red Army.
17 February	First fighting between Polish army and Red Army at Bereza Kartuska in Belarus.
5 March	Lenin moves Russian capital from Petrograd to Moscow.
15–16 April	Polish army begins first offensive against Red Army in Belarus.
1 July	Polish army begins Minsk offensive in Belarus.
3 July	Denikin's Volunteer Army begins march on Moscow.
17 July	Poles push Ukrainian Galician Army out of Galicia.
October	Yudenich's forces are routed.

1920

3 January   Polish and Latvian armies launch Operation *Winter* to capture Daugavpils.

27 January   Boris M. Shaposhnikov's Vistula plan presented to Lenin.

4 March   Polish army begins offensive to seize rail junction at Mozyr.

March   Denikin's army retreats into Crimea.

25 April   Polish Kiev operation begins.

7 May   Polish troops occupy Kiev.

14 May   Western Front launches first Belarussian offensive.

26 May   South-Western Front launches Kiev counter-offensive.

1 June   Polish army launches Belarussian counter-offensive.

5 June   First Horse Army makes major breakthrough south of Kiev.

4 July   Western Front begins major offensive in Belarus.

11 July   Entente proposes the Curzon Line.

13 August   Red Army begins attacks against Warsaw Bridgehead.

16 August   Piłsudski launches counter-offensive from the Wieprz River.

20 August   Mikhail Tukhachevskiy orders general retreat of the Western Front.

31 August   First Horse Army defeated at Komarów, forced to retreat.

26 September   Poles take Grodno, Tukhachevskiy orders retreat two days later.

8 October   Lucjan Żeligowski takes Wilno from Lithuania.

15 October   Poles occupy Minsk.

1921

21 March   Treaty of Riga signed, ending Russo-Polish War.

OPPOSING COMMANDERS

RED ARMY

As head of the Bolshevik Party, **Lenin** (**Vladimir Ilyich Ulyanov**) made most major strategic decisions concerning the Red Army. Central direction of the Red Army was entrusted to the Revolutionary Military Council of the Republics (*Revolyutsionny Voyenny Soviet Respubliki* – RVSR) with **Leon Trotsky** (**Lev Davidovich Bronstein**) as its chairman. Trotsky strongly shaped the organization and expansion of the Red Army in 1918 from a ragtag and incompetent militia into a formidable military force. One

Leon Trotsky, head of the Revolutionary Military Committee of the Republic.

of his key decisions was to incorporate trained military commanders from the former Imperial Russian Army into the Red Army as military specialists (*voenspets*) while teaming them with Bolshevik overseers. Besides providing the Red Army with competent officers, this also discouraged apolitical officers from joining the various White Russian armies. This policy started the practice of dual command in the Soviet military system with the actions of the military officers overseen by reliable party activists. All key orders had to be signed by the commissars. Under the Red Guards, traditional Russian ranks were abolished. Instead, functional designations were used: for example, *Komkorp* (corps commander), *Komdiv* (divisional commander), *Kompolk* (regimental commander), etc.

Sergey S. Kamenev, head of the Red Army's high command.

Mikhail N. Tukhachevskiy, commander of the Western Front.

The head of the High Command of the Armed Forces of the Republic (Glavkom VSR) since July 1919 was **Sergey S. Kamenev**. He had followed a professional military career, serving as an infantry regimental commander during World War I and chief of staff of the XV Army Corps in late 1917. He volunteered his services to the Red Army in early 1918, serving initially on the Western Front against the Germans, and in 1919 in Siberia against Admiral Aleksandr Kolchak's army. His skilled leadership in the fighting against Kolchak brought him to the attention of Lenin, who selected him to lead the Red Army in July 1919 in place of Jukums Vācietis, who had fallen out of favour with the RVSR.

Two fronts were committed to the Polish campaign in 1920. The Western Front was led by **Mikhail Tukhachevskiy**. He served as a lieutenant in the elite Semyonovsky Guards Regiment at the start of World War I and was captured in February 1915. He escaped from German camps four times, and was finally thrown into the Ingolstadt fortress in Bavaria, reserved for hard-case prisoners. His cellmate was another troublemaker, French Captain Charles de Gaulle. He managed a fifth escape and returned to Russia in September 1917. He joined the Bolshevik Party in 1918, and in May 1918 served as a commissar in the defence of the Moscow region. In spite of the fact that he came from a gentry family, he was regarded by senior party officials as a committed Bolshevik. At the age of only 26, he was assigned to command the First Army on the Eastern Front against Kolchak's army and the Czechoslovak Legion from June 1918 to January 1919. He subsequently commanded the Eighth Army on the Southern Front. Between February and April 1920, he led the Caucasus Front during the defeat of Denikin's army. His outstanding leadership in the battles against Denikin led to his appointment to lead the Western Front, and he was regarded by Lenin as one of the top Bolshevik commanders.

The South-Western Front was commanded by **Aleksander I. Yegorev**. Born in 1883, he joined the Russian army in 1902 and became a lieutenant in 1905. Of peasant background, he joined the Socialist Revolutionary Party in 1904. During World War I, he rose in rank to lieutenant-colonel and was wounded five times. He

joined the Bolshevik Party in July 1918 and became involved in the early efforts to create the Red Army. In August 1918, he commanded units in the fighting in Central Asia. From December 1918 to May 1919, Yegorev commanded the Tenth Army during the defence of Tsaritsyn, where he became acquainted with the RVSR representative, Iosef Stalin. Yegorov was decorated with the Order of the Red Banner for his leadership in the battle on the Sal River on 25 May 1919 against Denikin's troops. He was appointed to lead the Southern Front on 26 September 1919. The Southern Front was renamed the South-Western Front on 10 January 1920 due to its shift in focus to Ukraine.

Lenin assigned one of the principal Bolshevik leaders, **Iosef Stalin (Ioseb Jughashvili)**, as a representative of the RVSR to Ukraine. Stalin had served in much the same role a year earlier, where he became acquainted with another Bolshevik, **Kliment Voroshilov**, serving as the deputy commander of the Southern Front. The two men became close allies in intrigues against army leaders Trotsky and Kamenev, and they would come to form the core of what became known as the Tsaritsyn Circle.

Aleksander I. Yegorev, commander of the South-Western Front.

The third member of the Tsaritsyn Circle was **Semën Budënniy**. Unlike Stalin, Budënniy was a professional soldier, serving in the army since the age of 20 in 1903. He was a highly decorated cavalry sergeant-major in World War I. He joined Boris Dumenko's 1st Peasant's Socialist Punitive Cavalry Regiment, which gradually evolved into a brigade and then into the 4th Cavalry Division. Budënniy led the division after May 1919 and first became acquainted with Stalin and Voroshilov during the defence of Tsaritsyn, later renamed Stalingrad. The 4th and 6th Cavalry divisions were consolidated into the I Horse Corps under Boris Dumenko in September 1919. When Dumenko was wounded, Budënniy was assigned to lead the enlarged First Horse Army (Pervaya Konnaya Armiya). During 1920, it usually consisted of four cavalry divisions. This army became the shock force of the Red Army in the 1919–20 campaigns.

Iosef V. Stalin, RVSR representative of the South-Western Front.

The other essential cavalry formation in 1920 was the III Cavalry Corps with Tukhachevskiy's Western Front. This was led by **Gaya Dmitrevich Gai (Gayk Bzhishkyan)**. His father was a prominent Armenian revolutionary who fled from Tsarist police to Iran in the 1880s. His first cavalry command came in March 1920, when he led the 1st Caucasus Cavalry Division on the Southern Front. On the basis of his

ABOVE LEFT
Semën Budënniy, commander of the First Horse Army on the South-Western Front.

ABOVE RIGHT
Gaya D. Gai (Bzhishkyan), commander of the III Cavalry Corps of the Fourth Army on the Western Front during the Battle of Warsaw.

superior leadership in the spring campaigns, he was assigned to lead the III Cavalry Corps during the Warsaw campaign.

Command and control of the Red Army was modern, based around a radio network established for the Russian army during World War I with French technical assistance. Radio communications were critical during the Polish campaign, since the telegraph network in the Borderlands had been badly smashed up during the incessant fighting in the region. While the Red Army's radio network might seem to be an arcane technical detail, it had profound consequences in 1920. The Red Army suffered from a shortage of trained radio operators, and it relied on a relatively simple encryption system. As is discussed in more detail below, the Poles quickly appreciated the Red Army reliance on radio and this became a vital source of signals intelligence about Red Army strength and plans.

POLISH ARMY

Józef Piłsudski was the central figure in the resurrection of modern Poland, much like Mannerheim in Finland and Atatürk in Turkey. He was born in 1867 into a gentry family; his father had taken part in the 1863 insurrection against Russian rule. He attended the same gymnasium in Wilno as Feliks Dzierżyński, later head of the Soviet VCheKa political police. He became active in socialist politics and studied medicine at the University of Kharkov in Ukraine. Piłsudski and his brother were arrested in 1887 in connection with a plot against the Tsar; Lenin's brother was hanged for his involvement in the same plot. After Siberian exile, he returned to Wilno and became a prominent member in the early Polish Socialist Party (*Polska Partia Socjalistyczna* – PPS) and publisher of its underground newspaper. He was arrested again in 1900, escaping a St Petersburg jail in 1901 by feigning insanity. He became involved in the armed struggle against Russian rule in 1904 as a founder of the Combat Organization of the PPS, and helped organize the general strike in the Polish provinces during the 1905 Russian Revolution. In 1906, with some Austrian aid, he began forming Polish paramilitary units. These groups conducted bank and train robberies against the Russians. While living in Kraków before the war, one of his neighbours down the street was Vladimir Lenin, who was serving as a correspondent for the *Pravda* newspaper; they are not known to have met.

Marshal Józef Piłsudski, Polish leader and head of the army during the 1917–21 fighting.

At the start of World War I in 1914, Piłsudski led the Riflemen's Association (*Związek Strzelecki*). This formed the basis for the Polish Legions (*Legiony Polskie*) allied to the Austro-Hungarian Army. Piłsudski personally led its 1st Brigade in combat and the force eventually grew to about 25,000 troops. On 5 November 1916, Germany created a Polish puppet state called the Regency Kingdom of Poland, and Austro-Hungary announced plans to transfer the Polish Legions to German command. Some troops, including Piłsudski, refused and were imprisoned. Piłsudski was released from Magdeburg Prison and was appointed the commander-in-chief of the new Polish army on 11 November 1918. He was subsequently asked to head the new provisional government, so serving as both military and political leader of the new Poland.

The leadership of the Polish army between 1918 and 1920 was composed of officers who had served in the Polish Legions, as well as officers from the

FAR LEFT
General Tadeusz Rozwadowski, chief of staff of the Polish army in the summer of 1920.

FAR RIGHT
General Józef Dowbor-Muśnicki, leader of the Wielkopolska Army and one of Piłsudski's chief political rivals in the army.

RIGHT
General Stanisław Szeptycki was a brigade commander in the Polish Legion in 1917 as seen here. He subsequently served as commander of the Lithuanian-Belarussian Division in 1919 and the Northern Front in 1920.

FAR RIGHT
Lieutenant-General Józef Haller, organizer of the Blue Army in France in 1918, and head of the Northern Front in the summer of 1920.

Austro-Hungarian, Russian and German armies. Many of Piłsudski's closest associates had served with him in the Legions, such as his former chief of staff **Kazimierz Sosnkowski**, brigade commanders **Józef Haller, Zygmunt Zieliński** and **Stanisław Szeptycki**, as well as younger commanders such as **Edward Śmigły-Rydz** and **Władysław Sikorski**. Many of the older commanders had served in the Tsarist army. For example, **Józef Dowbor-Muśnicki** served in Manchuria in the Russo-Japanese War and led the Russian First Army in 1917. **Lucjan Żeligowski** served in the 1905 Russo-Japanese War, and was a lieutenant-colonel and commander of an Imperial Russian rifle regiment. **Wacław Iwaszkiewicz** served in the Russian army during the siege of Port Arthur in 1905 and was a highly decorated officer between 1914 and 1917, rising to the Russian rank of major-general. Other officers, such as **Tadeusz Rozwadowski**, served in the Austro-Hungarian army. Rozwadowski was an artillery specialist, and by 1917 rose in rank to *Feldmarschall-Leutnant*.

RIGHT
General Edward Śmigły-Rydz led the Polish operation to capture Kiev in May 1920, as well as the Strike Group during the Warsaw counter-offensive in August 1920.

FAR RIGHT
General Kazimierz Sosnkowski was overall commander of the Warsaw defences in August 1920.

OPPOSING FORCES

RED ARMY

The Red Army, or more formally the Workers' and Peasants' Red Army (*Raboche Krestyanskaya Krasnaya Armiya* – RKKA), was the outgrowth of the original Red Guards organized in November 1917 as the military arm of the new Bolshevik government in Petrograd. It began as voluntary, politically motivated militias and guerrilla bands, with commanders selected by their own men. The early militias had little battlefield stamina against conventional armies. Under Trotsky's leadership, the RKKA reverted back to conventional army organization.

The Red Army was organized in similar fashion to the Imperial Russian Army, based around rifle and cavalry divisions. As was traditionally the case in this period, divisional strength reports were usually given in terms of bayonets and sabres – in other words, the fighting strength of the division. This total was inevitably smaller than the division's total ration strength, which included the non-combat elements of the division.

In March 1918, plans were unveiled for the formation of 88 infantry divisions. Later in the year, the infantry divisions were renamed as rifle divisions (*pekhotnaya/strelkovaya*). The Red Army issued standard tables of organization and equipment (*shtat*). The November 1918 rifle division was organized into three rifle brigades, each with three regiments and a ration strength of about 58,000 men, a combat strength of 36,265 men and 24,340 horses.

In reality, Red Army rifle divisions were seldom more than a fraction of the authorized tables. For example, the average divisional strength in March 1920 was only 4,675 bayonets, 535 sabres, 28 field guns and 50 machine guns, roughly one-eighth of authorized strength. By January 1919, the Red Army had a combat strength of 350,000 bayonets, 17,000 sabres, 13,000 machine guns and 2,000 guns organized into 28 rifle divisions and six cavalry divisions.

A parade of a Red Army rifle regiment in Kharkov, Ukraine in 1920. Russian infantry frequently had to make do without boots in 1920, resorting to wrappings or other improvised coverings.

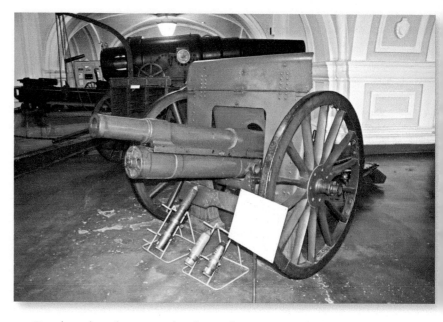

The backbone of the Red Army's artillery was the Putilov 3in. (76mm) M.02 divisional gun. This example is preserved at the Central Artillery and Engineer Museum in St Petersburg.

Cavalry played a central role in the 1919–20 fighting. Compared to Western Europe, troop and weapons densities in these conflicts were very low. As a result of the low levels of firepower, cavalry remained the vital arm of manoeuvre.

By the summer of 1920, the Red Army had expanded to 64 rifle and 14 cavalry divisions. At the end of 1920, it had an overall strength of 5.5 million men, of whom 2,456,000 were in the deployed army with a fighting strength of 778,000 men; and 2,971,000 were deployed in the rear area, including training, occupation and service units. The Red Army's tooth-to-tail ratio was about 1:12 due to the large number of army personnel committed to the rear area; the Polish ratio was much leaner at 1:7.

At the time of the Battle of Warsaw in 1920, about half of Red Army combat strength was deployed against Poland, including 23 divisions on the Western Front and 11 divisions on the South-West Front. The remaining units were located on the Northern Front near Petrograd (five divisions), in the Crimea against Wrangel (five divisions), in the Caucasus, Central Asia and Siberia (14 divisions), and in reserve (12 divisions).

Armament of the Red Army was the same as the Imperial Russian Army and many of the Russian arms and ammunition factories continued to produce new equipment. Some war booty equipment was used, mainly British artillery and tanks captured from the White Russian armies.

The lack of good roads in the Borderlands increased the military importance of railways. Most of the major campaigns were fought along the railways, and railway

The Air Fleet of the Red Army operated over 200 aircraft on the Western Front in the summer of 1920. This is pilot Frants Shishkovskiy of the 14th Fighter Detachment in front of his Nieuport 24bis on the Western Front in May 1920.

junctions were major military objectives. The importance of the railways led to the widespread use of armoured trains in these conflicts. These were the Eastern European equivalent of tanks and provided protected, mobile firepower. They were often used as shock force during an attack, and were also valuable to conduct rearguard operations during retreats. They were, in effect, small combined-arms forces, usually incorporating their own cavalry and infantry dismounts to extend their battlefield footprint. By 1920, nearly one-tenth of Red Army artillery was concentrated on the armoured trains. Ideally, each rifle or cavalry division had a few armoured trains. About 300 armoured trains were created by the Red Army between 1918 and 1920, with a peak strength of about 105 at the end of 1920.

Armoured cars were also widely used in 1919 and 1920, but they were confined to the roads due to their lack of cross-country mobility. Of the 605 manufactured in Russia or imported between 1914 and 1920, about 215 were in service with the Red Army in 1919. The Red Army captured tanks from the White armies, but they played no significant role in operations against Poland.

The Red Army was supported by a modest aviation force, the Red Aviation Fleet. On paper, each rifle and cavalry division was allotted a detachment of four aircraft, though actual strength varied widely. During the Polish campaign, the detachments were used primarily for army cooperation missions such as scouting and liaison. The aircraft had a low sortie rate due to the mechanical exhaustion of most of the aircraft and a shortage of replacement engines and repair parts.

The extensive waterways in the Pripyat area and the lack of roads encouraged the use of 'brown-water navies' in the region, as well as in some parts of Ukraine. The most important of these in the 1920 fighting was the Dnieper Flotilla, subordinated to the South-Western Front. Gunboats provided mobile firepower and escorted transport ships that were used to move troops and supplies.

Over 600 armoured cars had been built in Russia or imported from 1914 to 1920. The Russkiy-Ostin was one of the last types in production, with 52 built in 1918 and 1919 at the Putilov and Izhorskiy factories in Petrograd on imported Austin chassis. This example, *Vrag Kapitala* (Enemy of Capital), built in June 1919, is preserved at the Central Artillery and Engineer Museum in St Petersburg. It served in the 1st Armoured Car Detachment alongside another Ostin, *Stenka Razin*, shown elsewhere in this book.

NEW TOOLS OF REVOLUTIONARY WAR: AN ARMOURED TRAIN IN COMBAT (PP. 26–27)

The armoured trains built in the later years of World War I were highly prized due to their quality compared to the many improvised armoured trains. The story of these trains encapsulates the vicissitudes of the war in the Borderlands. This particular train (1) served in six different armies between 1917 and 1920.

In 1917, the Greter i Krivanek (GiK) yard in Kiev was working on four armoured trains for the Imperial Russian Army. They each had an armoured locomotive and two artillery cars, fitted with two 76mm gun turrets (2), four Maxim machine-gun turrets (3) and four more machine guns in side embrasures (4).

The No. 4 GiK train was in Odessa in December 1917 for repairs and was eventually commandeered by Skoropadsky's Hetmanate army. When the Hetmanate was overthrown by Petliura's Directorate in November 1918, this train entered service with the Assault Corps (*Osadyi Korpus*) of the DA-UNR as the *Sichovyi Strilets* (*Sich Riflemen*). The train fought against the Bolsheviks in early 1919 but was captured near Korosten in April 1919. In Bolshevik service, it was part of the armoured train detachment of the 1st Ukrainian Soviet Rifle Division, and was called *Kommunista Korostenkovo Raiona* (*Communists of the Korosten Region*). It was commanded by Lukyan M. Tabukashvili, who won the Order of

Red Banner for his leadership of the train in combat. The same Bolshevik armoured train detachment had one or more of the other GiK trains, including *Karl Libknekht*. Between late July and August 1919, several of these trains were captured by the 4th Zolochiv Brigade of the Galician UHA, including *Kommunista Korostenkovo Raiona* near Starokonstantinov station. It was renamed as *Cherepak* (*Turtle*) by the Galician troops. Eventually it was realized to have been the earlier DA-UNR train *Sichovyi Strilets* and so it was returned to Petliura's troops. It was renamed *Vilna Ukraina* (*Free Ukraine*, **5**) after another train with this name that had been lost previously in the war. On 16 September 1919, it fought against Denikin's forces near Mardarivka station, where it was damaged. In October 1919, under commander Lieutenant Semyon Loshchenko, it fought with the Denikin armoured train *Korshun* (*Kite*). It was subsequently damaged in combat and left at Proskurov station for repairs. It was captured by the Polish 45th Kresowa Rifles at Miropol station on 7 December 1919. The Polish army used this train to create *Postrach II* (*Terror No. 2*) that fought in Ukraine in early 1920. Surviving bits of GiK armoured trains were used to assemble later Polish trains including the *General Listowski*.

RED ARMY IN THE POLISH THEATRE, AUGUST 1920

WESTERN FRONT (KOMZAPFRONT MIKHAIL N. TUKHACHEVSKIY)

Third Army (Komandarm Vladimir S. Lazarevich)
5th Rifle Division (K. I. Gryunshteyn)
6th Rifle Division (A. A. Storozhenko)
21st Rifle Division (G. I. Ovchinnikov)
56th Rifle Division (K. N. Annenkov)
Fourth Army (Komandarm Yevgeniy N. Sergeyev[2])
12th Rifle Division (A. G. Reva)
18th Rifle Division (I. F. Kuprianov)
53rd Rifle Division (K. P. Shcherbakov)
54th Rifle Division (V. N. Shubin)
143rd Brigade (48th Rifle Division)
164th Brigade (55th Rifle Division) (M. I. Rozen)
III Horse Corps (KomKor Gaya D. Gai)
10th Cavalry Division (N. D. Tomin)
15th Cavalry Division (V. I. Matuzenko)
Fifteenth Army (Komandarm Avgust I. Kork)
4th Rifle Division (V. I. Solodukhin)
11th Rifle Division (M. K. Simonov)
16th Rifle Division (S. P. Medvedovskiy)
33rd Rifle Division (O. A. Stigga)
Sixteenth Army (Komandarm Nikolai V. Sollogub)
2nd Rifle Division (R. V. Longva)
8th Rifle Division (V. M. Smirnov)
10th Rifle Division (A. E. Dauman)
17th Rifle Division (K. P. Nevezhin)
27th Rifle Division (V. K. Putna)

2   From 31 July 1920, Aleksandr D. Shuvayev.

Mozyr Group (Komdiv Tikhon S. Khvesin)
57th Rifle Division (N. Z. Mikita-Kolyada)
139th Brigade (47th Rifle Division)

SOUTH-WESTERN FRONT[3] (KOMYUGZAPFRONT ALEKSANDER I. YEGOREV)

Twelfth Army (Komandarm Sergey A. Mezhenikov)
7th Rifle Division (A. G. Golikov)
24th Rifle Division (V. I. Pavlovskiy)
25th Rifle Division (A. N. Bakhtin)
44th Rifle Division (I. N. Duboboy)
58th Rifle Division (V. V. Popov)
17th Cavalry Division (less elements) (A. K. Ilyushin)
Fourteenth Army (Komandarm Ieronim P. Uborevich)
41st Rifle Division (Zh. F. Zonberg)
45th Rifle Division (I. E. Yakir)
47th Rifle Division (P. A. Solodukhin)
60th Rifle Division (P. S. Ivanov)
8th Cavalry Division (V. M. Primakov)
1st Independent Cavalry Brigade
3rd Brigade (17th Cavalry Division)
First Horse Army (Komandarm Semën Budënniy)
4th Cavalry Division (F. M. Letunov)
5th Cavalry Division (Ya. F. Balakhonov)
6th Cavalry Division (S. K. Timoshenko)
11th Cavalry Division (N. P. Vishnevskiy)
14th Cavalry Division (E. M. Ravikovich)
Separate Cavalry Brigade

3   List does not include Thirteenth Army in Crimea.

POLISH ARMY

The Polish army was created out of multiple strands, from Polish troops serving in the former Russian, German and Austro-Hungarian armies, as well as Piłsudski's Polish Legions and self-defence militias created in 1918 and early 1919 in the border skirmishing. The new Polish army (*Wojsko Polskie*) was formally created on 11 November 1918. At the time, it had about 9,000 troops, rising to about 70,000 by January 1919, 110,000 in February 1919, 270,000 in May 1919, 600,000 by the end of 1919 and 780,000 men at the time of the Battle of Warsaw in August 1920.

In June 1917, the French army had agreed to create a Polish army in France, formed at first from Polish prisoners of war from the German army and Polish immigrants in France, and later opened up to volunteers from overseas, mainly the United States. It was variously called the Haller Army after its leader, Józef Haller, or the Blue Army after the colour of its

A Wielkopolska infantry regiment on parade. There were some regional differences in uniforms, such as the higher *Rogatywka* (square field cap) worn by the units raised in western Poland.

A machine-gun platoon of the 1st Wilno Rifle Regiment with Major Stanisław Bobiatyński seated in the centre. This detachment is armed with two French Hotchkiss modèle 1914 8mm machine guns and two German Schwarzlose water-cooled machine guns.

French uniforms. The Haller Army arrived in Poland from France between April and June 1919. Four divisions formed from Polish troops in the Tsarist army under General Żeligowski arrived from Odessa in June 1919.

In late 1919, the army was organized into 21 infantry divisions and seven cavalry brigades, rising to 23 infantry divisions and nine cavalry brigades a year later. Infantry divisions had two brigades, and generally three regiments per brigade. It was common for the infantry divisions to be divided up for missions, with brigade-sized formations dubbed 'groups'. Larger extemporized formations made up of more than a single division were called operational groups (*Grupa operacyjna*) rather than corps.

Poland had little military industry and initially was dependent on weapons found on Polish territory. In 1919, efforts began to purchase weapons abroad. The main source of supply was from France. Although

The Polish army deployed its 1st Tank Regiment during the 1919–20 fighting, equipped with 120 French Renault FT tanks. This particular tank was captured by the Red Army during the 1920 fighting, and donated to the Afghan army in the late 1920s. It was recovered from Kabul in 2002 and restored in Poland, currently residing in the Army Museum in Warsaw. (Wojciech Łuczak)

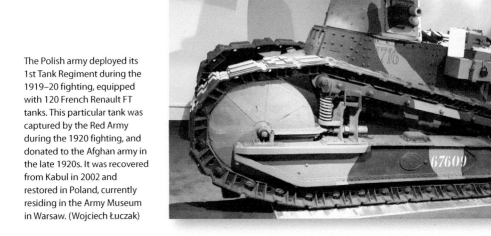

A large fraction of Polish artillery came from France. This is a Canon de 155 C modèle 1917 Schneider, with General Haller evident in the centre of the picture.

a significant number of Russian infantry weapons was available in early 1919, these fell out of favour during the course of the war due to problems with ammunition supply. At war's end, the army had about 600,000 rifles and carbines, of which about half were French, a third German and the remainder mostly Austro-Hungarian. The situation with machine guns was somewhat different, with French machine guns only 13 per cent, German 76 per cent and the remainder Austro-Hungarian and Russian.

The artillery branch had the greatest difficulty in formation due to the shortage of cannon and ammunition. The most common weapon was the ubiquitous Russian 76mm M.02 divisional gun. The first large import order went to Italy for 120 75mm M.06 field guns and a variety of larger weapons, along with associated ammunition. Both the Russian and Italian artillery declined in importance after 1919 due to ammunition shortages. The arrival of the Haller Army brought with it a large complement of modern French artillery. France subsequently sold or transferred to Poland 1,130 cannon by the end of 1919, with the 75mm M.1897 becoming the standard Polish field gun. In late 1920, the Polish army had 1,324 cannon, of which 69 per cent were French, 20 per cent Russian, 6 per cent German and 5 per cent Austrian.

In spite of Poland's long cavalry tradition, Piłsudski was not enthused about a large cavalry branch, feeling that cavalry had not proven its worth in World War I. Attitudes changed after the encounters with the First Horse Army in the spring of 1920, and the cavalry branch was expanded. By the end of the war, the Polish army had 30 cavalry regiments.

The Haller Army was accompanied by its own tank regiment, equipped with 120 Renault FT light tanks. This regiment was

Armoured trains were widely used in the 1918–20 fighting. This is *Pociąg Pancerny Nr. 1 Piłsudczyk*, which was created in 1918 from an Austro-Hungarian armoured train in the Kraków area. It saw extensive service in the fighting for Lwów in 1919 and in other theatres in 1920 and 1921. It is seen here during the Kiev campaign in 1920.

Many armoured trains built in 1919 and 1920 used improvised protection. This example of an assault wagon built in the Poznań area was based on an ordinary goods wagon with a second wooden wall inside. The gap between the two wooden walls was filled with concrete. The machine-gun embrasures were made from steel. (Wojciech Łuczak)

usually deployed as separate companies or battalions. As elsewhere in the region, Poland eventually fielded a substantial armoured train force. In total, Poland built about 80 armoured trains, including the construction of about 60 armoured locomotives and 300 armoured railcars. They also captured 37 armoured trains between 1918 and 1920, including 31 Bolshevik armoured trains and smaller numbers of Austro-Hungarian, Ukrainian, German and Lithuanian trains. The Polish army had seven armoured trains at the end of 1918, 31 at the end of 1919 and a peak strength of 43 around the time of the Battle of Warsaw in 1920. The Polish armoured car force was relatively small; it included a few captured Russian and German armoured cars, and small numbers of improvised armoured cars. The lack of interest in armoured cars was due mainly to their poor cross-country mobility.

This Nieuport 24 was captured by the Poles at Wilno from the Red Army's 3rd Artillery Aviation Detachment. It was put back into service with the Polish 4th Aviation Squadron and is seen here in Lida, Belarus on 15 June 1919 being flown by Lieutenant A. Jurkiewicz. The winged devil insignia was part of the original Bolshevik markings and was retained when captured, with the Polish national *Szachownica* (Checkerboard) insignia painted over the original red stars.

POLISH ARMY, AUGUST 1920

NORTHERN FRONT (GENERAL JÓZEF HALLER)

Fifth Army (Major-General Władysław Sikorski)
9th Infantry Division (Colonel Aleksander Narbutt-Łuczyński)
17th Infantry Division (Lieutenant-General Aleksander Osiński)
18th Infantry Division (Lieutenant-General Franciszek Krajowski)
22nd (Volunteer) Division (Lieutenant-Colonel Adam Koc)

First Army (Major-General Franciszek Latinik)
8th Infantry Division (Brigadier-General Stanisław Burhardt-Bukacki)
10th Infantry Division (Lieutenant-General Lucjan Żeligowski)
11th Infantry Division (Colonel Bolesław Jaźwiński)
15th Infantry Division (Brigadier-General Władysław Jung)
1st Lithuanian-Belarussian Division (Lieutenant-General Władysław Bejnar)

Second Army (Major-General Bolesław Roja)
2nd Legion Infantry Division (Colonel Michał Żymierski)
4th Infantry Division (Colonel Stanisław Kaliszek)

CENTRAL FRONT (MARSHAL JÓZEF PIŁSUDSKI)

Fourth Army (Major-General Leonard Skierski)
14th Infantry Division (Lieutenant-General Daniel Konarzewski)

16th Infantry Division (Major-General Kazimierz Ładoś)
21st Mountain Infantry Division (Colonel Andrzej Galica)

Strike Group (Major-General Edward Śmigły-Rydz)
1st Legion Infantry Division (Brigadier-General Stefan Dąb-Biernacki)
3rd Legion Infantry Division (Lieutenant-General Leon Berbecki)
4th Mounted Brigade (Colonel Gustaw K. Orlicz-Dreszer)

Third Army (Major-General Zygmunt Zieliński)
6th Infantry Division (Lieutenant-General Mieczysław Linde)
7th Infantry Division (Lieutenant-General Karol Schubert)
Don Cossack Brigade (Colonel Alexander I. Salnikov)

SOUTHERN FRONT (LIEUTENANT-GENERAL WACŁAW IWASZKIEWICZ)

Sixth Army (Major-General Władysław Jędrzejewski)
1st Mounted Division (Colonel Juliusz Rómmel)
13th Infantry Division (Lieutenant-General Stanisław Haller)

Ukrainian Regular Army (General Mykhailo Omelianovych-Pavlenko)
(see below for details)

As in the case of artillery, Poland's air force was slow to develop due to a lack of aircraft. Some were purchased in 1919, including ten Ansaldo Balilla fighters from Italy and 48 Albatros D.III (Oeffag) from Austria. Once again, France became the main source of supply including Breguet 14A2 light bombers. At peak strength in early 1920, the air force had about 130 combat aircraft. The large number of types and the challenging field conditions made it difficult to keep more than half operational at any given time.

Poland operated a small brown-water navy in the Pripyat marshlands, called the Pinsk Flotilla. Many of its vessels were captured from the Russians.

One of Poland's little-known advantages in the 1919–20 war was a small but efficient signals intelligence effort. The Austro-Hungarian army had operated a radio intelligence service against Russia between 1914 and 1918, and many Polish officers were recruited due to their language skills. These

The most famous Polish aviation unit was the American volunteer 7th Kościuszko Squadron that served mainly in Galicia and Ukraine. Several of the pilots are seen here in front of one of their Ansaldo A.1 Balilla fighters. On the wing (left to right) are Władysław Konopka and Kenneth M. Murray. On the ground are Jerzy Weber, Antoni Poznański, Zbigniew Orzechowski, Edward C. Corsi, George M. Crawford, John C. Speaks, Elliott W. Chess, Earl F. Evans, John I. Maitland, Aleksander Seńkowski and Thomas H. Garlick.

Simon Petliura (left), head of the Ukrainian Directorate, confers with General Edward Śmigły-Rydz (right) on 10 May 1920 following the capture of Kiev by their joint forces.

experienced Polish officers set up a Cypher Office (*Biuro Szyfrów* – BS) under the intelligence office of the General Staff in May 1919. This office began to regularly decrypt Russian radio traffic in August 1919, and by 1920, was often reading the messages in near real time. This operation expanded during the course of the war, and included radio signals collection, radio direction-finding and message deciphering. During the 1920 campaign, the signals intelligence effort was fruitful, since the Red Army relied principally on radio communications at divisional level and above. The Red Army encipherment programme proved more vulnerable than the previous Russian army programme since there were shortages of trained operators, and encryption security was lax. The Polish army was able to determine the location of many Red Army divisions during the course of the campaign, as well as order of battle and many key operational messages. In general, the Polish signals intelligence effort was most successful against the South-West Front, which was obliged to use radio since the local telegraph network had been torn up by continual warfare in Ukraine. Another fruitful source of intelligence was the Dnieper Flotilla, which exercised poor radio security and often retransmitted whole operational orders to its scattered vessels.

UKRAINIAN ARMY

The near destruction of Petliura's Dieva Armiya-UNR to the typhus epidemic in late 1919 forced the UNR government to form an alliance with Poland, even though it meant acceding to Polish territorial demands in Volynia and East Galicia. The Polish government agreed to provide military supplies to the DA-UNR. The 6th Division, named after the disbanded Sich Rifle formations, was created at the Łancut prisoner-of-war camp from POWs and troops of the DA-UNR who had been interned by the Polish army. This

Ataman Simon Petliura, in the dark uniform at the far left, reviews a unit of the Regular Army of the Ukrainian People's Republic (DA-UNR) near Tarnopol (Ternopil) at the time of the Kiev operation.

DA-UNR REGULAR ARMY (GENERAL MYKHAILO OMELIANOVYCH-PAVLENKO)

1st Zaporozhian Infantry Division (Colonel Andrii Hulyi-Hulenko)
2nd Volynian Division (General Oleksander Zahroskyi)
3rd Iron Infantry Division (Colonel Oleksander Udovychenko)
4th Kiev Infantry Division (General Iurii Tiutiunnyk)

5th Kherson Infantry Division (Colonel A. Dolud)
6th Sich Rifle Infantry Division (Colonel Marko Bezruchko)
1st Cavalry Division (General Ivan Omelianovych-Pavlenko)

division, commanded by Colonel Marko Bezruchko, was moved to Brest for training. It was the only Ukrainian division ready for the April operation against Kiev and served as part of the Polish Third Army.

The 2nd Division, commanded by Colonel Oleksander Udovychenko, was raised near Kamenets-Podolsk, mainly from existing DA-UNR troops. During the Kiev operation, the 2nd Division was only able to deploy a separate detachment under Colonel Pavlo Shandruk, numbering about 350 men. The 2nd Division reverted to its earlier name of the 3rd Iron Division in May 1920.

A formal alliance between Poland and Ukraine was signed on 21 April, followed by secret military protocols on 24 April 1920. By late April 1920, the DA-UNR only managed to deploy about 4,000 troops for the Kiev operation, since the remaining units had not been adequately supplied or armed. The other divisions were gradually built up through the course of the spring and early summer and gradually deployed in the defence of Ukraine. Through November 1920, the Polish Sixth Army in Ukraine provided Ukrainian forces with 30,000 rifles, 298 machine guns, 38 field guns and six heavy guns, and 40,000 uniforms.

Three of the early leaders of the Ukrainian Galician Army: (left to right) Ivan Bobersky, Dmytro Vitovsky and Lonhyn Tsegelsky. Vitovsky organized the initial capture of Lviv in November 1918 and subsequently became the war minister of the Western Ukrainian People's Republic (ZUNR).

OPPOSING PLANS

RED ARMY

Conflict between the Red Army and the Polish army remained at a simmer at the end of 1919. The main focus of the Red Army in early 1920 remained the White Russian armies, most notably White Russian forces in Crimea and the Caucasus. These units were now under the command of Baron Pëtr Wrangel, who had taken over command from Denikin after the defeat of the Volunteer Army in the autumn of 1919.

The defeats of the two principal White Russian threats in the autumn of 1919 prompted Lenin to contemplate the missions of the Red Army in 1920. In a speech to Ninth All-Russia Conference of the Communist Party on 20 September 1920, he described the situation at the end of 1919: 'We faced a new task. The defensive period of the war with worldwide imperialism was over, and we had the obligation to exploit the military situation to launch an offensive war.'

By December 1919, Lenin's focus had turned to Poland, since he regarded it as 'a buffer between Germany and Russia, the last state … in the hands of international imperialism against Russia. She is the linchpin of the whole Treaty of Versailles. The modern imperialist world rests on the Treaty of Versailles … by extracting [Poland] we break up the entire Versailles peace.' Lenin viewed Soviet Poland as a stepping stone to spur revolution in Germany, Hungary and perhaps even Britain. Lenin also planned to bring Poland back into the Russian embrace.

In December 1919, Lenin assigned the task of developing a plan to capture Poland to Boris M. Shaposhnikov, the head of the operational division of the Field Staff of the RVSR. Shaposhnikov studied earlier campaigns between Russia and Poland, and in particular the 1830–31 war. As in the case of the 1831 campaign, Shaposhnikov's plan favoured an approach on Warsaw via the Smolensk Gate, with the main thrust emanating from the western bank of the Dvina around Polotsk. A secondary operation would be conducted by the South-Western Front from Ukraine. This was apparently prompted by Lenin, who felt that a large Red Army force could use Galicia as a springboard into Hungary to foment revolution.

On 27 January 1920, Glavkom Sergey S. Kamenev provided Trotsky with a basic assessment of the balance of forces in the west, including Shaposhnikov's preliminary plan, which envisioned the start of a campaign against Poland in April 1920. This was formally sanctioned by the Politburo later that day.

Some Bolshevik officials, including war commissar Trotsky and foreign minister Georgiy Chicherin, urged that steps should be taken to avoid the appearance of Russia starting the war. By initiating a 'peace offensive', no matter how insincere, the pretense could be created of an aggressive Poland provoking Russia into war. The main aim of the peace offensive was to create a wedge between Poland and the Entente. Chicherin launched the peace offensive on 28 January 1920 with a renewal of offers to Warsaw to begin negotiations.

While the peace negotiations attracted worldwide attention, the plans for a Polish campaign began to take shape in secret. Lenin formally approved Shaposhnikov's plans on 14 February 1920. The timing of the attack was dependent on several factors, including the weather, rebuilding the Red Army in the wake of the 1919 campaigns and shifting the Red Army's main concentrations towards the west. The harsh winter months were unsuitable for starting a campaign and the early spring could complicate the advance if the weather was wet and muddy.

The process of reinforcing the Polish theatre began in early February 1920 with the transfer of the 44th and 60th Rifle divisions. Between January and February 1920, the Red Army in the Polish theatre increased from a ration strength of 80,000 to 134,000. Combat strength increased from 27,000 on 1 January 1920 to 93,500 troops on 25 April 1920 at the start of the Polish Kiev operation. Between January 1920 and April 1920, the Red Army shifted 20 divisions and five brigades to the Polish theatre, of which 12 divisions went to the Western Front, and eight divisions to the South-Western Front. The Shaposhnikov plan anticipated the need for a strength of 225,000 bayonets and 20,000 sabres to conduct the operation against Poland, and so divisions were shifted west through the summer.

Red Army strength in the Polish theatre, 1 August 1920

	Combatant strength	Ration strength
Western Front	136,292	382,071
South-Western Front	147,875	282,507
Total	284,167	664,578

POLISH ARMY

Poland's strategic objectives were largely shaped by Józef Piłsudski. His personal experiences led him to distrust Russia, Tsarist or Bolshevik. Piłsudski sought a Russia weakened by the loss of its prosperous western provinces. These same western provinces, especially the Baltic States, Belarus and Ukraine, could form a federation that would shield Poland from Russia. Piłsudski hoped that France and Britain would support his schemes to serve as a bulwark against Soviet Russia.

Piłsudski's objectives were not universally shared. Roman Dmowski, head of Poland's largest political party the National Democrats, was opposed to such a federative scheme. Dmowski did not want to become entangled in Belarussian and Ukrainian politics. Dmowski's strategic vision was more fervently anti-German than anti-Russian, and his political powerbase was in the western Wielkopolska region. Due to his diplomatic role in Western Europe in 1917 and 1918 in support of the new Polish state, Dmowski's view of a more compact Polish state was better known to the Entente than Piłsudski's federative vision, and had won the support of Britain and France.

By the end of 1919, Piłsudski's strategic vision had been confounded by the foreign policies of Poland's potential Borderland allies. Two of the nearest neighbours, Lithuania and Galician Ukraine, were adamantly anti-Polish. The orientation of Galician Ukraine became irrelevant by the end of 1919, since its army had been overwhelmed and largely destroyed by the 1919 battles and epidemics; its territory was mostly under Polish control. Belarus had been a major disappointment for Piłsudski, since attempts to create a viable state with its own army had proven to be completely ephemeral.

For Piłsudski's federative scheme, the big question in 1920 was the fate of Right-Bank Ukraine. Petliura had little to lose in promoting a Polish–Ukrainian alliance in early 1920, since without Polish aid, his movement would be little more than a shadow government-in-exile.

Due to the success of the Polish army's signals intelligence operation, Piłsudski had a fairly detailed appreciation of the Red Army's order of battle. In spite of Chicherin's 'peace offensive', the evidence pointed to a likely Red Army operation against Poland sometime in the spring of 1920. Piłsudski felt that a Bolshevik attack via the Smolensk Gate was the most likely, since Bolshevik power was strongest in the Petrograd–Moscow–Orël area. In the modern era, the logistical network along the Moscow–Warsaw corridor was far superior to the Kiev–Warsaw corridor.

Piłsudski decided to stage a pre-emptive operation into Right-Bank Ukraine in the early spring, before the Red Army had the opportunity to complete its reinforcement of the Polish theatre for its own offensive into Poland. The goal of this operation was to establish Petliura's UNR back in control. The other option, a strike into Belarus via the Smolensk Gate, had no strategic appeal. The weather in the early spring would be unhelpful due to the rain and mud, and Red Army forces in the region were denser and better situated along river defence lines. Weather in Ukraine in April 1920 would be more favourable than in the north, and Red Army defences in the south were less formidable.

The attitude of the Entente was critical to the Polish plan, since the Polish army was heavily dependent on France for arms and equipment. The Poles began to put out feelers to the French government in December 1919 about potential military action against the Bolsheviks in 1920. French and British policy towards Russia was in a state of flux at the end of 1919 due to the defeat of the two principal White Russian armies backed by the Entente. In December, Britain's Prime Minister David Lloyd George and French Premier Georges Clemenceau met in London. Clemenceau made it clear that France now viewed the anti-Bolshevik crusade of the past year to have been a waste. Instead, he argued that Germany remained the main threat and that Russia should be contained by erecting 'a barbed-wire entanglement', with Poland and Romania constituting the principal barriers against Bolshevik troublemaking in central Europe. Lloyd George sought a new policy to end the civil war and to reach an accommodation with the Bolsheviks. As a result, Britain ended the naval blockade of Russia in January 1920 and began steps to resume trade. In February, the Entente agreed to put an end to military aid to Denikin and the White Russian cause. Many in the British government viewed the Polish question through the lens of Britain's recent troubles with Ireland and were not at all sympathetic to Polish separatism. They viewed independent Poland as a French project and believed it would remain an obstacle to Lloyd George's mercantilist rapprochement with Russia.

Alexandre Millerand succeeded Clemenceau in January 1920. His view of the Soviet peace offensive in 1920 was far more pessimistic than the British view. He believed Moscow's peace offensive was only a manoeuvre to give the Bolsheviks a breathing space until an appropriate moment arrived to attack Poland. On 22 February 1920, the French government agreed to an 80 million franc export of ammunition to Poland.

In early 1920, the French general staff was shown a Polish draft plan for an offensive to create a new defence line along the Dvina–Dnieper rivers. They responded unfavourably, warning the Poles that they were underestimating Bolshevik military power and overextending themselves with too ambitious a scheme. However, French policy remained equivocal, neither approving Piłsudski's forthcoming attack, nor formally disapproving of it. Millerand remained deeply suspicious of Moscow and left it up to the Poles to decide on their own course of action. France was Poland's primary military benefactor, and so the opinion of Paris carried much more weight than that of London. In the absence of any firm opposition from either Paris or London, Piłsudski felt that he had tacit Entente support for the forthcoming Kiev operation.

THE CAMPAIGN

OPENING MOVES

Piłsudski planned two small operations as a prelude to the main Kiev operation. In the north-east, Piłsudski wanted to eject the Bolsheviks from the region near the city of Daugavpils. This was part of a broader political effort to draw Latvia into a political alliance with Poland, as well as to create a corridor between Poland and Latvia, thereby isolating Lithuania from Russia. The Latvian army had been pre-occupied defending the country against the German-sponsored Western Army under Colonel Pavel M. Bermondt-Avalov, which was not finally overwhelmed until early December 1919. An alliance was signed between Poland and Latvia on 30 December 1919.

Command of Operation *Winter* was entrusted to one of Piłsudski's closest confidantes, Edward Śmigły-Rydz, leading an operational group of the 1st and 3rd Legion Infantry divisions totalling about 30,000 Polish soldiers and supported by two dozen Renault FT tanks. The main Latvian component was its 3rd Infantry Division with a strength of about 10,000 troops. The opposing Bolshevik Fifteenth Army had about three understrength rifle divisions in the area with a total strength of 13,490 bayonets and 177 sabres.

Operation *Winter* began on 3 January 1920 with the Polish troops crossing the frozen Daugava River in a blizzard with temperatures of -35° C (-31° F). The Bolshevik garrison was surprised and quickly overcome. The Polish units continued to push forward, and repulsed a Bolshevik counter-attack on 7 January 1920. Once the area was free of Bolshevik forces, the Polish army withdrew.

The next operation, entrusted to the Polesie Group under Władysław Sikorski, aimed to wrest control of Mozyr from the Bolshevik South-Western Front. Mozyr was a major

Polish troops of the 5th Legion Regiment of Śmigły-Rydz's operational group move into Daugavpils (Dyneburg) on 3 January 1920 as part of Operation *Winter*. This early winter campaign was intended to push the Bolsheviks out of south-eastern Latvia as part of a broader effort to form a military alliance between Latvia and Poland.

railway junction on the north–south line that connected the Western Front and South-Western Front. Control of Mozyr would prevent the Red Army from transferring troops between the two fronts in subsequent campaigns. Furthermore, the city was located at the bend in the Pripyat River, and so control would prevent the Russians from sending their river flotillas westwards. Sikorski's units had a strength of 8,500 troops and two armoured trains, while opposing Bolshevik forces numbered 4,500 troops and six armoured trains.

The Mozyr attack was launched in the pre-dawn hours of 4 March 1920, while the rivers and swamps in the area were still frozen. Sikorski's forces first took the railway junction of Kalenkowicze behind the Bolshevik lines, isolating Mozyr. As a result, Mozyr quickly fell later in the day. The importance of the Mozyr–Kalenkowicze railway junctions was not lost on the Red Army and a series of counter-attacks was launched, starting with an unsuccessful attack on 8 and 9 March. The front was reinforced and on 16 March, another major attack was launched, without success. As a result, the Poles controlled the rail junctions until the start of the spring campaign.

THE KIEV OPERATION

The Kiev operation began on 25 April 1920. The Polish forces consisted of three field armies: the Third Army under direct high command control, the Second Army commanded by General Antoni Listowski and the Sixth Army under General Wacław Iwaszkiewicz. At the time, the Polish army committed a little under half its strength, 52,000 combat troops, to the Kiev operation.

The portion of Yegorev's South-Western Front in the Polish theatre in late April were Komarm Sergey Mezhenikov's Twelfth Army with a combat strength of 8,509 bayonets and 1,588 sabres, and Komarm Ieronim Uborevich's Fourteenth Army with 4,866 bayonets and 691 sabres. In total on 20 April 1920, the South-Western Front had a ration strength of 66,573 and a combat strength of 15,654 troops. The units of the South-Western Front were badly overextended with divisions covering frontlines of 50–75km.

A portion of the South-Western Front was tied down with anti-partisan operations against the persistent peasant uprisings in Ukraine, instigated in part by Petliura's UNR. Much of the anti-partisan fighting was conducted by the paramilitary VOKR (*Voenizirovannaya Okhrana* – Armed Guards) brigades, and in April 1920 there were about 5,000 of these troops in action in Ukraine aside from regular army units conducting these missions. Armed bands probably numbered over 12,000 at this time, and were a persistent menace through all of the Bolshevik rear areas.

A group portrait of the 4th (Machine-Gun) Company, I/43rd Kresowa Rifle Regiment at Szepetówka (Shepetivka) in Ukraine on 19 March 1920 prior to the Kiev operation. This regiment was at the centre of the defence against the First Horse Army in late May 1920.

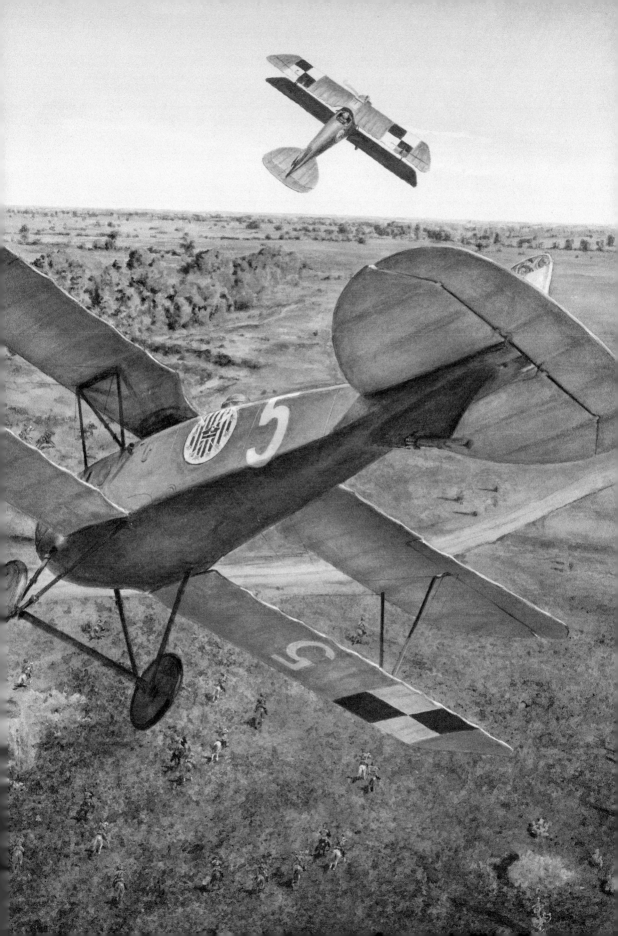

BUDËNNIY'S SCOURGE: AN ALBATROSS SORTIE BY THE KOŚCIUSZKO SQUADRON, 1920 (PP. 42–43)

Massed cavalry was especially vulnerable to air attack. The 7th Kościuszko Squadron saw extensive combat against Budënniy's First Horse Army and was one of the first Polish aviation units to spot its approach in March 1920. This squadron was unusual: it was formed in late 1919 around a core of American volunteer pilots. The squadron was initially equipped with D.III (Oeffg) Albatros fighters, a version of the famous German fighter built in Austria. It was later supplemented with Italian Ansaldo Balilla fighters.

This scene shows an attack on Bolshevik cavalry (**1**) in the spring of 1920. The aircraft in the foreground (**2**) was piloted by Captain Merian Cooper, who is better known for his post-war career as a Hollywood film director, including the popular film *King Kong*. The aircraft to its left (**3**) was piloted by the squadron commander, Major Cedric Fauntleroy, who had served with Eddie Rickenbacker's 94th Fighter Squadron during World War I. The 7th Squadron first deployed to Galicia in March 1920 and was eventually assigned to the Sixth Army. One of its primary missions was to fly deep reconnaissance missions to locate Bolshevik formations. In late May, the squadron began to pick up the first evidence of a large Bolshevik cavalry formation approaching the Kiev area. The squadron also proved exceptionally valuable after the breakthrough of the First Horse Army, since they were able to track the progress of Budënniy's forces deep behind Polish lines. During the ensuing battles near Kiev, the squadron conducted a number of attack missions against Budënniy's First Horse Army. On one occasion, after running out of machine-gun ammunition, the aircraft attacked the cavalry by trying to strike the riders with the undercarriage of their aircraft. The fighters were so disruptive of cavalry operations that Budënniy's headquarters requested that Moscow dispatch special anti-aircraft units. In the event, a shortage of replacement aircraft and spare parts greatly limited the sortie rate of the squadron later in the summer.

Moscow planned to substantially reinforce the South-Western Front for the planned attack on Poland, but fighting in the Caucasus and Crimea delayed these plans. One of the major reinforcements for the South-Western Front was Budënniy's First Horse Army, assigned to the mission in early March 1920. At the time, the army was in the Caucasus Mountains about 1,000km from the Dnieper, fighting against the remnants of the White Russian army. Budënniy and Voroshilov travelled to Moscow on 30 March to discuss the plans with Glavkom Kamenev. The Red Army staff wanted to transfer the army to Ukraine using railway transport. Budënniy firmly opposed this, arguing that the railways were in poor condition and that a large portion of the horses would become debilitated in the process. He argued instead that it should march on horseback to Ukraine. This long interval also permitted the addition of more units to the army, so that by the time it reached Ukraine, it numbered over 16,500 sabres, nearly double its strength from earlier in 1920. This was accomplished in part by combing out POW camps for Cossack troops who had been serving under Denikin and Wrangel. When the Polish Kiev operation started on 25 April, the South-Western Front commander asked Moscow to speed up the transfer by using rail transport for at least one cavalry division. Budënniy again resisted this attempt to break up his force, and as a result, no cavalry reinforcements were sent to Kiev in late April. It took the First Horse Army seven weeks to make the 1,000km journey, starting at Maikop in early April and reaching Uman, south of Kiev, on 24 May 1920.

The orphan Galician UHA, abandoned by Denikin in January 1920, joined the Bolsheviks as the Red Galician Army in February 1920. Although the units were strengthened to about 11,000 men with additional Ukrainian troops, the commitment of these units to Moscow was dubious. Due to lingering uncertainty over the loyalty of these troops, the brigades had been dispersed into three Bolshevik rifle divisions of the Fourteenth Army. Ukrainians allied to the Poles infiltrated the units and began anti-Bolshevik agitation. There were mutinies in two of the three Galician UHA brigades in the days before the Polish attack. The 2nd Galician Brigade mutinied on 23 April, fighting against other regiments of the 45th Rifle Division. The

Troops of the Polish 6th Legion Infantry Regiment during the Kiev operation in late April 1920.

POLISH

Third Army
1. 9th Infantry Division
2. 2nd Cavalry Brigade
3. Rybak Group
   1st Highland Rifle Brigade
   41st Infantry Regiment
   7th Mounted Brigade
4. 4th Infantry Division

Second Army
Śmigły-Rydz Operational Group
5. 7th Infantry Division
6. 3rd Mounted Brigade
7. 1st Legion Infantry Division
8. Mounted Division
9. 6th Ukrainian Sich Rifle Division
10. 15th Infantry Division
11. 13th Infantry Division

Sixth Army
12. 18th Infantry Division
13. 12th Infantry Division
14. 5th Infantry Division
15. Shandruk Detachment,
    2nd Ukrainian Division

EVENTS

1. 23 April: Captain Iulian Holovinskyi's 2nd Galician Brigade with the 45th Rifle Division mutinies, fighting against other regiments of the 45th Rifle Division.

2. 24 April: Captain Osyp Stanimir's 3rd Galician Brigade mutinies, fighting the Russian regiments of the 41st Rifle Division.

3. 25 April: The Polish army begins the Kiev operation, focusing most heavily on the Twelfth Army along the main Korosten to Kiev railway line.

4. The 7th Rifle Division, deployed on the Korosten–Kiev railway, stages a bayonet charge against a Polish cavalry brigade outside Malin and suffers 40 per cent casualties.

5. The 44th Rifle Division attempts to hold the rail junction at Kozyatin against the Polish 5th and 15th Infantry divisions, but after a day's fighting, is overrun and disperses.

6. Mezhenikov's Twelfth Army headquarters attempts to consolidate the retreating units behind a river defence line west of Kiev along the Irpen River, and begins to deploy a reserve of about 2,000 troops.

7. 25 April: the Revolutionary Military Council of the Twelfth Army decides to evacuate the civilians from Kiev over the course of the following week.

8. 4–5 May: the Polish forces temporarily halt to reconfigure the Second and Third armies for the final assault.

9. 1 May: Moscow orders Kiev to be held at all costs and begins to dispatch reinforcements to the city.

10. 1 May: Mezhenikov attempts to stage a counter-attack against the Polish spearhead using the remaining troops of the 7th Rifle Division, but can barely muster 600 men.

11. Night, 5/6 May: The Polish infantry attack resumes on Kiev's western defences.

12. 6 May: Mezhenikov's headquarters orders the Twelfth Army to evacuate Kiev.

13. 6 May: Colonel Alfred Bisanz's 1st Galician Brigade mutinies against the remainder of the 44th Rifle Division.

14. 6 May: A Polish cavalry patrol enters the city and finds it is not defended. Polish forces enter and occupy Kiev on 7 May.

THE KIEV OPERATION, 25 APRIL–10 MAY 1920

The Kiev operation began on 25 April 1920. Poland committed almost half of its forces – three field armies, totalling 52,000 troops – to the operation.

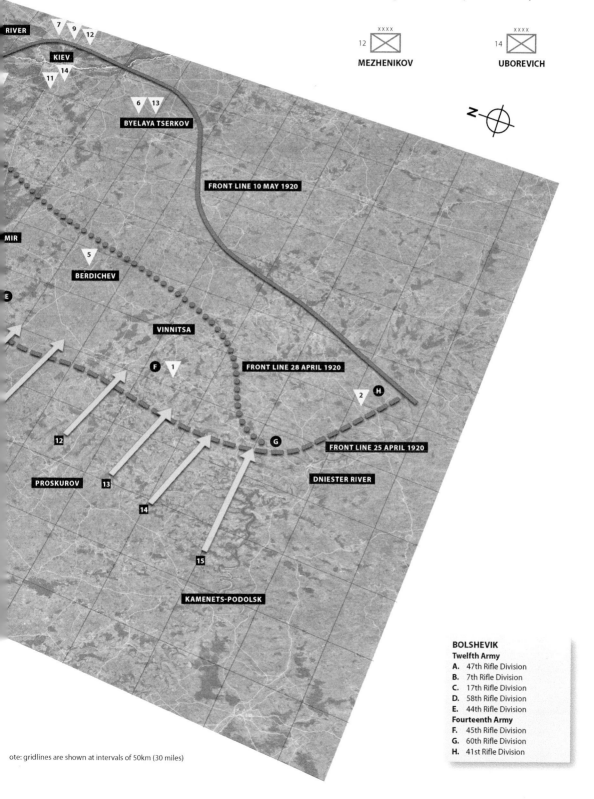

RIVER

7 9 12

KIEV

14

11

6 13

BYELAYA TSERKOV

FRONT LINE 10 MAY 1920

MIR

5

BERDICHEV

E

VINNITSA

F 1

FRONT LINE 28 APRIL 1920

2 H

12

G

FRONT LINE 25 APRIL 1920

PROSKUROV 13

DNIESTER RIVER

14

15

KAMENETS-PODOLSK

12 xxxx MEZHENIKOV

14 xxxx UBOREVICH

N

BOLSHEVIK
Twelfth Army
A. 47th Rifle Division
B. 7th Rifle Division
C. 17th Rifle Division
D. 58th Rifle Division
E. 44th Rifle Division
Fourteenth Army
F. 45th Rifle Division
G. 60th Rifle Division
H. 41st Rifle Division

ote: gridlines are shown at intervals of 50km (30 miles)

Ataman Simon Petliura reviews the troops of the 6th Sich Rifle Division in Kiev in May 1920 along with the division's senior staff. To his immediate left is Colonel Marko Bezruchko, the divisional commander. The officer with the prominent moustache between them is Colonel Mikola Ianchevskyi of the staff headquarters.

mutiny spread to the 3rd Galician Brigade the following day, disrupting the 41st Rifle Division. The 1st Galician Brigade, part of the 44th Rifle Division, remained loyal to the Bolsheviks for the time being, not finally switching sides until 6 May. The mutinies not only disrupted much of the Fourteenth Army, but it obliged Yegorev to move in additional units to suppress the turncoats.

The Polish army struck on 25 April, while this chaos was still distracting the two rifle divisions. The Polish attacks fell most heavily on the Mezhenikov's Twelfth Army, especially along the main railway line through Korosten to Kiev. Some Bolshevik rifle divisions put up a stiff fight in several of the towns. The 7th Rifle Division, deployed on the Korosten–Kiev railway, staged a bayonet charge against a Polish cavalry brigade outside Malin and suffered 40 per cent casualties. The 44th Division attempted to hold the rail junction at Kazatin against the Polish 5th and 15th Infantry divisions, but after a day's fighting, was overrun and dispersed. In two days of fighting, Mezhenikov's Twelfth Army was largely overwhelmed and lost touch with Yegorev's headquarters.

Mezhenikov sent out a string of orders to subordinate divisions trying to establish new defence lines during the first days of the campaign. The orders arrived after the divisions had already retreated past intended defence lines. After a few days of fighting, many of the messages did not get through at all, as Ukrainian partisan units had been given specific instructions to rip down telegraph wires behind Bolshevik lines. Mezhenikov's headquarters attempted to consolidate the retreating units behind a river defence line west of Kiev along the Irpen River. Between the start of the Polish offensive and 5 May, the Twelfth Army's fighting strength fell from 8,509 to 2,511 bayonets. In contrast to the predicament of the Twelfth Army, Uborevich's Fourteenth Army was hit by more modest forces and was able to retreat in better order.

The Polish forces did not have enough cavalry to trap the retreating Bolshevik units, and so failed to secure a decisive defeat of the South-Western Front. Piłsudski believed that the Twelfth Army would stiffly defend Kiev. As a result, on 4 and 5 May, the Polish forces temporarily halted to reconfigure the Second and Third armies for the final assault.

On 1 May, Moscow ordered Kiev to be held at all costs and began to dispatch reinforcements to the city. Mezhenikov attempted to stage a counter-attack against the Polish spearhead using the remaining troops of the 7th Rifle Division. However, the counter-attack force could barely muster 600 men and had no effect.

Piłsudski ordered two Polish cavalry brigades to cross over the Dnieper and approach Kiev from the rear, planning to trap any remaining forces. The Polish infantry attack resumed on the night of 5/6 May and began attacking the defences on the west side of the city. With the Bolshevik defences outside the city faltering, at noon on 6 May, Mezhenikov's headquarters ordered the Twelfth Army to evacuate Kiev. A Polish cavalry patrol entered the city on 6 May and found it undefended. Polish infantry entered and occupied Kiev on 7 May.

In the aftermath of the capture of Kiev, the Polish army halted and established defensive positions. A bridgehead was established over the Dnieper near Kiev, and defences forward of the Zhmerinka–Kiev railway line further to the south. Piłsudski hoped that Petliura would be able to rally Ukrainian popular sentiment to the cause and build up Ukrainian army strength sufficiently so that Polish troops could be withdrawn. In the face of the famine, epidemics and general war-weariness in Right-Bank Ukraine, the Ukrainian political and military response was deeply disappointing to Piłsudski.

General Edward Śmigły-Rydz reviews the troops of the Third Army in Kiev on 11 May 1920. The officer on the horse behind him is Colonel Julius Rómmel, who commanded the Third Army's artillery, and later commanded the 1st Mounted Division in the concluding cavalry battle at Komarów.

The quick Polish victory in the Kiev operation was far from being an unalloyed success. Piłsudski had miscalculated the political and diplomatic impact of the operation in Western Europe. Lloyd George's government in Britain was highly critical of the attack; the Millerand government less so. Lenin and the Bolshevik leadership were pleased by the outcome of the campaign, which they viewed as a tactical military failure but a strategic political success. Military losses had been modest by civil war standards, about 30,000 men. Kiev had changed hands so often in the previous two years that its capture was of no long-term consequence. The Polish Kiev operation fitted into the Bolshevik peace propaganda that cloaked the forthcoming offensive into Poland. Moscow stepped up its political agitation in Western Europe, encouraging British and German dockyard workers to refrain from loading cargoes destined for Poland. 'Hands off Russia' became the political slogan of the trade unions and the left in Western Europe through the summer of 1920, with Poland cast as the aggressive and rapacious villain in this political drama.

THE FIRST BELARUS OFFENSIVE

The Polish attack on Kiev forced the Red Army to accelerate its plans for an offensive through Belarus. The Western Front facing Poland had been gradually strengthened since early February 1920 when Moscow signed a ceasefire with Latvia and a treaty with Estonia. This allowed the transfer of units from the Seventh Army around Petrograd to the Polish theatre and permitted the consolidation of the entire Fifteenth Army against Poland.

The deployment of many of the best Red Army combat units to the Crimea and Caucasus to deal with Wrangel's White Russian armies in early 1920 delayed the start of the offensive, which had originally been scheduled to begin in April 1920. Lenin wanted a more experienced commander to lead the Western Front assault, and Mikhail Tukhachevskiy was recalled from his command of the Caucasus Front and replaced Vladimir M. Gittis on 29 April.

When Tukhachevskiy visited the existing deployments on the Western Front, he was dismayed by the poor quality of the units that had been stationed there over the past few years. He later wrote: 'Those which were already on the Western Front were not very reliable. They had been spread out over long fronts for several years and had become exhausted and demoralized by continual raids and harassing operations by the more enterprising Polish troops ... Moreover, no serious active operations had been organized on either side ... In conjunction with the reverses we had suffered at the hands of the Poles in the previous year, there was an atmosphere of anxiety and timidity in these units.'

Tukhachevskiy requested the transfer of veteran rifle divisions from other fronts with better fighting spirit. Most of the fresh divisions were concentrated in Kork's Fifteenth Army, while Sollogub's Sixteenth Army kept the less satisfactory units. As a result of the Polish advance on Kiev, Moscow wanted to initiate the Western Front offensive, even if its forces in the sector were still too weak to assure a definitive success. As a result, on 5 May, Tukhachevskiy ordered the attack to commence on 14 May 1920.

The geography of the northern warpath offered two principal corridors: the Smolensk Gate via Polotsk, and a second approach via Igumen. Although Igumen offered a better set of bridges for crossing the Berezina, the area to its south-west was complicated by forested and swampy areas and a lack of roads. The route via the Smolensk Gate was selected as the focus of the attack. However, there were only a few bridges over the Dvina at Polotsk, and the best ones were damaged. This would have created a narrow bottleneck for the Fifteenth Army if this had been the starting point for the offensive. Instead, Kamenev and Tukhachevskiy decided to attack out of the Vitebsk area against the badly overstretched Polish 8th Infantry Division. The Bolshevik Fifteenth Army would be the main strike force, advancing with five rifle divisions against the Polish 8th Infantry Division, while another of its divisions attacked the neighbouring 1st Lithuanian-Belarussian Division. On penetrating the Polish defences and reaching the main Polotsk–Minsk railway line, the Fifteenth Army would make a sharp left turn southwards

KomZapFront Mikhail Tukhachevskiy reviews a Red Army regiment on its way to the Western Front in the summer of 1920.

On its way to the Polish front is the training unit of the Red Army's 27th Rifle Division, which served with Sollogub's Sixteenth Army.

towards Minsk, accessing the Smolensk Gate from behind. The neighbouring Sixteenth Army to the south would push out westwards towards Igumen and Borisov along the Orsha–Borisov–Minsk railway line. A small Northern Group was left along the Dvina on either side of Polotsk to tie down Polish defences.

Tukhachevskiy later calculated the strength of the Western Front as 92,393 combatants with the bulk of the forces, 55,896 troops, in the Fifteenth Army. His later report suggests that opposing Polish forces were roughly similar, although he only lists 56,500 Polish troops in the entire region, including units to the south in Polesie. This was an exaggeration. Other Bolshevik accounts suggest that he significantly undercounted his forces, omitting numerous reserves and other units. In the event, the main contest between Kork's Fifteenth Army against the Polish First Army's 8th and 1st Lithuanian-Belarussian divisions pitted about 56,000 combatants against 9,100. Furthermore, the 8th Infantry Division was grossly overextended along a 70km defence line.

The Polish deployment in Belarus consisted of a thin screen of units along the front with reserves behind. Piłsudski was aware of the build-up of the Western Front and planned to launch a pre-emptive attack by the Fourth Army from the Polesie area northwards against the Bolshevik Sixteenth Army towards Zhlobin and Mogilev with the intention of disrupting the Bolshevik offensive. Piłsudski issued orders for this attack on 11 May 1920, with an intended start date of 17 May. In the event, this never took place, since Tukhachevskiy struck first.

Polish intelligence in Belarus was not as good as in Ukraine. The area had not been subjected to the same level of devastation as Ukraine and the telephone and telegraph network was in much better condition. As a result, most Bolshevik communication was conducted using these channels, which were not transparent to the Polish signals-intelligence network. The Poles did have reasonably good order of battle information based on traditional intelligence means, such as POW interrogations, but they did not have any insights into the timing or intentions of the Western Front high command.

Officers of a rifle regiment of the 1st Lithuanian-Belarussian Rifle Division. This unit served as part of the Polish First Army during the May 1920 fighting in Belarus.

When the Western Front launched its offensive on 14 May 1920, Kork's Fifteenth Army was able to overwhelm the overextended Polish First Army. Once the forward defences had been overrun, the 15th Cavalry Division was sent out to disrupt the retreat of the First Army and to capture or destroy the field army's headquarters; this effort largely failed. In the meantime, the weaker Sixteenth Army pushed westwards towards Borisov against the Polish Fourth Army, but without such dramatic results as the Fifteenth Army achieved further north. Over the next two weeks, Kork's Fifteenth Army was able to push the Poles back to the south-west, and to the outskirts of Minsk at its deepest penetration. The Bolshevik advance was slowed by very poor logistical preparations. Many divisions exhausted their supplies of ammunition and food in less than a week.

Although Piłsudski's planned pre-emptive strike had failed to materialize, it had led to the concentration of reserves in Belarus that could be used to counter-attack Tukhachevskiy's forces. General Sosnkowski was assigned to gather a Reserve Army on the north-western flank of the Polish line, while General Skierski's Fourth Army was instructed to concentrate the units that had been intended for the Polish attack on Zhlobin. A Northern Front headquarters under General Stanisław Szeptycki was created to manage the Polish forces in Belarus.

The Polish counter-attack began on 1 June from the northern and southern ends of the front, aimed at enveloping the Fifteenth Army spearheads. By this stage, the Fifteenth Army had become largely exhausted. For example, the 53rd Rifle Division of the Fifteenth Army had been reduced from 5,142 bayonets at the start of the offensive to fewer than 1,500; some accounts suggest only 580 bayonets. By 2 June, the Fifteenth Army had been halted and some units were forced to retreat. In a conversation on 4 June, Tukhachevskiy suggested that the Western Front should fall back to more defensible positions and replenish its dwindling manpower and supplies. Glavkom Kamenev firmly opposed this, and based on Lenin's instructions, told Tukhachevskiy to prepare to regroup and push forwards to Wilno. This was complete fantasy and the planned counter-attack did not materialize.

The fighting on 7 and 8 June made it clear to Moscow that no further advance by the Western Front was possible, and the Fifteenth Army withdrew behind the Auta River and took up a defensive posture. The three-week Western Front offensive in Belarus ended with few territorial gains for the Red Army. The Fifteenth Army had suffered casualties of over 12,000 troops, about a quarter of its combat strength. Figures for the Sixteenth Army are not known but were probably comparable. The fighting had been something of a shock for Tukhachevskiy, who found that the Polish army units were far more formidable than the slapdash White Russian units he was accustomed to fighting. The Polish formations, even when overwhelmed, tended to retreat in good order and not run away in panic.

Correspondingly, the Polish units of Szeptycki's Northern Front were alarmed by their encounters with the battle-hardened troops of the Fifteenth Army, who were very unlike the demoralized Red Army units they had become accustomed to fighting in Belarus over the previous year.

From the strategic perspective, the May offensive convinced both Tukhachevskiy and the Red Army command in Moscow that an improvised offensive against Poland was unlikely to succeed. In his report, Tukhachevskiy suggested that a force of about 290,000 troops would be needed; the May offensive had involved only about a third as many.

ATTACK OF THE FIRST HORSE ARMY

After its seven-week march from the Caucasus, Budënniy's First Horse Army arrived near Uman on 24 May. At the time, it numbered four cavalry divisions with a combat strength of 18,000 sabres. Supporting arms included 52 field guns, five armoured trains, eight armoured cars and an aviation detachment with 15 aircraft.

Opinions of Budënniy's cavalry were often extreme, from their legendary status in Stalinist Russia to the more jaundiced view of their opponents. Lieutenant-General Sir Adrian Carton De Wiart, holder of the Victoria Cross and a senior member of the British Military Mission to Poland, was not impressed. 'This Bolshevik force ... was largely composed of Cossacks. Cossacks are the most disappointing cavalry soldiers, for they have neither enough training nor enough discipline to make them efficient in modern warfare. What they lack in skill, they try to make up for in brutality and murder.' A Polish cavalry officer, Colonel Tadeusz Machalski, suggested: 'The Horse Army had more suggestive power than actual strength. It only possessed a few elite detachments, amounting to no more than two divisions. The rest were little more than "mounted riders"

A portrait of the military Soviet of the First Horse Army in May 1920. In the seated row (left to right) are Pavel V. Bakhturov, Semyon M. Timoshenko, RVSR representative Kliment Voroshilov, Komarm Semën Budënniy, S. A. Kotov, O. I. Gorodinkov and A. M. Detistov.

The breakthrough of First Horse Army, 29 May–13 June 1920

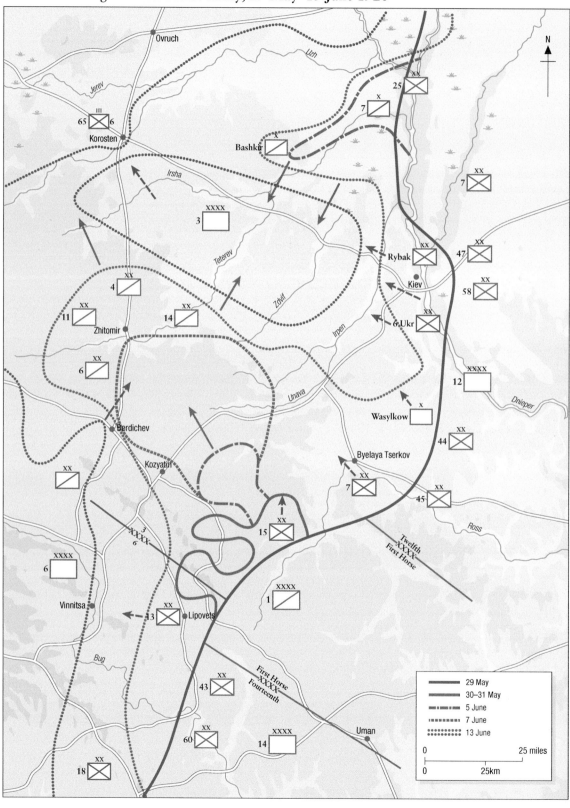

riding horses that should have never left the plow. This swarm of horsemen would raise gigantic dust-clouds on the horizon, blotting out everything for miles around, and giving the impression of a great, fast-moving and fantastic force pouring into every open gap, and finally igniting a feeling of utter impotence in the opposing ranks.' Trotsky was not convinced of the loyalty of the Horse Army, remarking at the time that 'wherever [Budënniy] leads his gang, they will follow. For the Reds today, for the Whites tomorrow.'

Piłsudski was not overly alarmed by the presence of the First Horse Army, because the performance of Bolshevik cavalry in the Polish theatre to date had been unimpressive. General Aleksander Karnicki, in command of the new Mounted Division (*Dywizija Jazdy*) in Ukraine, did not share this opinion. Karnicki had been assigned to the Polish liaison mission to Denikin's army in 1919 and he had seen at first hand what the Horse Army could do in the right circumstances. Karnicki was a former Tsarist cavalry general, and curiously enough, he had promoted Budënniy to corporal many years before.

Regardless of their precise military prowess, the arrival of the First Horse Army in Ukraine turned the tide of battle on the Polish front. Yegorev's South-Western Front at the time consisted of three field armies: Mezhenikov's Twelfth Army, Uborevich's Fourteenth Army and Budënniy's First Horse Army. The Front's ration strength was 377,250 men, of whom 62,160 were combatants. A portion of the rest were tied down with the incessant struggle against peasant uprisings. The South-Western Front also included the Dnieper Flotilla, a brown-water navy organized into two contingents with over 15 gunboats and a large number of transports, tugs and small river craft and its own marine force.

General Edward Śmigły-Rydz's Ukrainian Front consisted of General Zygmunt Zieliński's Third Army in the Kiev area and General Wacław Iwaszkiewicz's Sixth Army to the south. Besides the two field armies, the front also included Operational Group Słucz under General Jan Romer on its northern flank. The Ukrainian DA-UNR under General Mykhailo Omelianovych-Pavlenko was attached to the Sixth Army except for the 6th Sich Rifle Division, which remained with the Third Army in the Kiev area, serving as Petliura's presidential guard. The total ration strength of the Polish

One cavalry weapon ubiquitous to the cavalry fighting in 1919 and 1920 was the *tachanka*, a four-wheel cart adapted to carry a machine gun on the rear. This was the method used by the cavalry to include machine guns in mobile warfare. This is a view of a regiment of the First Horse Army in Ukraine in June 1920 with two *tachanka* machine-gun carts evident.

army south of Polesie was 156,500, of whom about 15,500 were Ukrainians. This was about half the size of the opposing South-Western Front.

The Polish defences in Ukraine were stretched very thinly, especially in the area south of Kiev. The situation was made worse by the decisions in late May to begin transferring divisions out of Ukraine to Belarus due to the fighting there. The Polish infantry divisions in Ukraine were assigned to hold a front line ten times those typical during World War I, often a hundred kilometres. Under such circumstances, linear trench defence was impossible. Instead, the Poles attempted to create a 'pearl necklace' of strongpoints, usually based on villages or hilltops. The space in between was covered by machine-gun and field-gun fire. Behind the line of strongpoints were reserve battalions.

Moscow's plan was the envelopment and destruction of the Polish Third Army in the Kiev area, followed by an exploitation phase aimed at propelling the Red Army past Lwów to Równe and Lublin. The attack on Kiev was assigned to Mezhenikov's Twelfth Army, which planned to tie down the Third Army in its bridgehead east of the Dnieper River, while operational groups under Aleksander Golikov and Iona Yakir enveloped the Polish positions from either side. Budënniy's First Horse Army was assigned to probe along the inter-army boundary to find a weak spot between the Polish Third and Sixth armies. Bolshevik intelligence was not very good, in large measure due to the Polish use of Ukrainian partisan units to screen the front from Bolshevik patrols. When issued the plan on 20 May, Budënniy complained about the lack of precision in explaining the disposition of opposing forces.

The Bolshevik Kiev campaign began on 26 May 1920, with infantry attacks on either side of Kiev. The Poles responded with aggressive infantry counter-attacks, and the Red Army failed to make serious inroads into the Kiev defences. An infantry raid against the Bolshevik 44th Rifle Division overran the divisional headquarters. After several days' fighting, Mezhenikov's Twelfth Army was forced to retreat and regroup.

The aviation detachment of the First Horse Army on the South-Western Front in June 1920. In the foreground are a pair of Airco DH.9 light bombers.

Budënniy moved all four of his cavalry divisions forwards, but due to the need to rest and replenish the cavalry divisions in the wake of their epic march from the Caucasus, they did not make serious contacts with the Polish defence line until 29 May. In addition, some of the cavalry divisions became distracted by skirmishes with the Ukrainian partisans. Once in contact with the main Polish defence line, Budënniy followed his usual tactic of pushing three divisions forwards with the fourth in reserve to exploit any gaps that were located.

Although railways moved most of the military supplies to forward depots, horse-drawn wagons were the backbone of the Red Army's logistics. Tukhachevskiy's Western Front had more than 30,000 carts in the summer of 1920. This is a supply column of the First Horse Army in 1920.

The battle did not start well for the Poles in this sector. On learning of Budënniy's approach from aerial reconnaissance on 24 May, the 13th Infantry Division planned to move their defences forwards to the Roska and Ros rivers further east. Orders were dispatched on 28 May, but when it became apparent that Budënniy was on the verge of attacking, the orders were rescinded. Unfortunately, the change of orders did not reach the 50th Kresowa Rifles. Their two forward battalions began advancing alone into the dark on the night of 28/29 March. Budënniy's attack started the same evening. The two battalions of the 50th Kresowa Rifles were overwhelmed by the 6th Cavalry Division. The Cossacks had been ordered not to take prisoners; the lead battalion was massacred, and the second battalion took severe losses.

The loss of the 50th Kresowa Rifles created a gap between the 43rd and 45th Kresowa rifles that the 6th Cavalry Division was quick to exploit, pushing to the north-west towards the critical rail junction at Kozyatin. The 6th Cavalry Division spent the day trying to expand the breach by pushing back its southern shoulder against the 45th Kresowa Rifles. In the process it lost a brigade staff and 300 prisoners on the first day of fighting, but managed to penetrate about 20km beyond the Polish forward line of battle. In response, the 13th Infantry Division created a counter-attack force under Colonel Antoni Szylling of the 44th Kresowa Rifles based around a reserve battalion that pinched off penetration at its base and forced the withdrawal of the 6th Cavalry Division on 31 May.

The attack by the 11th Cavalry Division against the 43rd Kresowa Rifles near Dhiunkov initially was ineffective, with the Red cavalry making disjointed and costly mounted attacks against the Polish strongpoints. The 4th Cavalry Division made a shallow penetration of the gap between the 43rd Kresowa Rifles and an isolated battalion of the 44th Kresowa Rifles near Novo-Khvastov. A deeper penetration was prevented by the arrival of a reserve Polish infantry battalion as well as a sally by regiments from General Karnicki's Mounted Division that erupted into a cavalry vs. cavalry battle near Volodarka. That night, the 4th Cavalry Division's 3rd Cossack Brigade, made up mostly of Cossacks formerly of Denikin's army, shot their political officers and defected to the Polish side. On 31 May, the 11th Cavalry Division

FIRST HORSE ARMY'S BREAKTHROUGH, MAY 1920 (PP. 58–59)

The arrival of Budënniy's First Horse Army around Uman in May 1920 played the central role in defeating the Polish army in Right-Bank Ukraine. The initial attacks at the end of May 1920 were repulsed with heavy losses to both sides. After a shift in tactics to subject Polish defences to more firepower, the First Horse Army was able to finally penetrate the main defence lines on 5 June 1920, precipitating a rout of the Polish Third Army from Kiev.

The Bolshevik cavalry, primarily based on Cossack regiments, fought almost entirely from horseback and shunned dismounted dragoon tactics. They wore traditional Cossack uniforms, though many of the troops took a liking to the new Bolshevik broadcloth helmet (*shlem sukonniy*, **1**) that became popularly called the 'Budënovka' after Budënniy due to its association with the First Horse Army. Their weapons were primarily the sabre and pistol, though some troops did use carbines and other weapons.

One of the tactical innovations during the Russian civil wars was the use of the *tachanka* (**2**). This was an ordinary four-wheel, horse-drawn carriage carrying a single Maxim machine gun. During assaults, the *tachankas* would be driven forward to set up a concentrated base of firepower to support the mounted attacks. During defensive operations, they could serve in the rearguard to discourage enemy pursuit. The First Horse Army had attached armoured trains and armoured cars for further fire support. There was an aviation detachment as well, though it suffered heavy losses in the early phase of the Kiev campaign, and so played a minimal role in the subsequent fighting.

pushed through the Polish lines between the 43rd and 44th Kresowa rifles, but were counter-attacked by General Jan Sawicki's 3rd Cavalry Brigade. By 1 June, the Polish lines had been largely restored and the Bolshevik cavalry pushed back.

The poor results of the first four days of fighting forced Budënniy to call a temporary halt to the attack on 2 June. At a meeting with his division commanders, all agreed that the casual mounted tactics that had been so successful against Denikin had proven too costly against the Poles. After resting and refitting, the First Horse Army returned to the battlefield on 5 June. All four divisions were concentrated to overwhelm the centre of the Polish 13th Infantry Division's defences. With no remaining reserves in this sector, the Polish defences were completely breached. The Bolshevik cavalry penetrated 20km behind the Polish defences and the First Horse Army reached the northern banks of the Rostavytsiya River, south-east of Koziatyn, by evening. This attack turned the tide of the conflict and gave the Red Army the strategic initiative in Ukraine.

Troops of the Red Army's 3rd International Rifle Regiment, commanded by the Hungarian Lajos Gavro. This was one of a number of Soviet units formed mainly from foreign Marxists in Russia. This regiment served on the South-Western Front in 1920, sometimes as part of the First Horse Army.

Kamenev instructed Budënniy to continue to push to the north-west to cut off the Polish Third Army. Instead, Yegorev sent Budënniy on cavalry raids towards Koziatyn, Zhitomir and Berdichev to cut behind the Polish Sixth Army further south. These raids diffused the power of the Horse Army and were blunted by counter-attacks by Karnicki's Mounted Division.

Attacks against the Polish Third Army around Kiev continued to be frustrated. To outflank the Kiev defences, Yegorev instructed Komdiv Aleksandr Golikov to form an assault group based around his 7th Rifle Division and supported by the 25th Rifle Division, the Bashkir Cavalry Brigade and other assorted forces that were landed across the Dnieper by the Dnieper Flotilla to attack towards the rail line at Malin, behind Polish lines. Yegorev's operational aim was to trap and destroy the Polish Third Army between the two Bolshevik forces.

Besides the First Horse Army, other cavalry formations served on the South-Western Front. This is a squadron of the Separate Bashkir Cavalry Brigade that served with Golikov's Assault Group fighting against the Polish Third Army during its retreat from Kiev.

By 10 June, Golikov's Assault Group had reached the Kiev–Korosten railway line with the 25th Rifle Division immediately to the west of Kiev, and the Bashkir Cavalry Brigade at Malin. The Yakir Group, consisting of the 44th and 45th Rifle divisions, pushed behind the Polish defences at Kiev from the south through the 7th Infantry Division. In the face of the encirclement threat, Śmigły-Rydz ordered a retreat from Kiev that day, moving along the railway line to Korosten to a new defence line along the Uzh River. Golikov's Assault Group had a fragile grip on the railway line and

his forces were pushed back by the retreating Poles. Budënniy was ordered to cut off the retreat, but his cavalry divisions were harassed by rearguard Polish cavalry regiments and he failed to make contact with the main Polish forces. As a result, the South-Western Front failed in its operational goal of encircling and destroying the Polish Third Army. Nonetheless, they had completely undermined the Polish–Ukrainian forces in Right-Bank Ukraine and forced their precipitous retreat.

Piłsudski realized the critical role that the First Horse Army had played in the defeat at Kiev and was determined to squash it. The Polish army was short of cavalry regiments and so he was forced to strip Szeptycki's Northern Front of cavalry to reinforce the weakened Mounted Division. This was attached to General Kazimierz Raszewski's Second Army, reformed in May 1920 to stabilize the Ukrainian front.

With the Polish forces in retreat, Budënniy used his usual tactics and sent the four divisions of the First Horse Army on a mission to find gaps in the Polish defences. On 26 June, the First Horse Army crossed the Uzh River, forcing the Poles to fall back to the Horyn River. Days later, Budënniy repeated the process, and the First Horse Army found a weak point along the Horyn on 2 July, heading for the district capital of Równe in Volynia. The Bolshevik cavalry surprised the Polish 3rd Legion Infantry Division, forcing it to withdraw. Budënniy set up his headquarters in the city, only to find it under attack by the Polish 3rd and 18th Infantry divisions on 7 and 8 June. Budënniy narrowly avoided capture, but the fight for the city ended on 10 June when the Polish army decided to pull back to a more defensible position along the Styr River. This was precipitated by the new Bolshevik Western Front offensive.

THE MAIN RED ARMY OFFENSIVE IN BELARUS

The Red Army had never intended for Ukraine to be the main contest in the war with Poland. Tukhachevskiy's 14 May offensive in Belarus was an improvised affair intended to take pressure off the South-Western Front in Ukraine. During the final three weeks of June 1920, Tukhachevskiy's Western Front underwent a massive build-up for its main offensive. One of the most important aspects of this effort was to substantially improve the logistical support of the Western Front that had proven so inadequate in the May offensive.

The orders for the offensive were issued to Tukhachevskiy on 20 June, with the start scheduled for 4 July 1920. In contrast to the May offensive, the July offensive included four field armies instead of two. Furthermore, there was a much more substantial cavalry force in the form of Gai's III Cavalry Corps, attached to the Fourth Army on the right (north) wing of the assault. The plan was to capture Warsaw by 12 August,

In the wake of the summer 1920 offensive, the Red Army established Proletarian Militias in Polish cities to take over control from local police forces. This is a Bolshevik militia patrol in Grajewo, a town north of Białystok. The militiaman here to the right is armed with a Russian Mosin-Nagant M1891 rifle.

a six-week advance of 750km. Tukhachevskiy's orders to the Western Front proclaimed: 'Over the corpse of White Poland lies the road to worldwide conflagration. Our bayonets will bring happiness and peace to the toiling masses of mankind. To the West! … On to Wilno, Minsk and Warsaw! Forward!'

At the time, the Western Front had a ration strength of 497,574, and a combat strength of 90,509 bayonets, 6,292 sabres and 595 field guns. Estimated Polish strength including deep reserves were 86,400 bayonets, 7,500 sabres and 188 light and 77 heavy guns. However, actual Polish strength at the front was only 33,400 bayonets, 4,100 sabres, 156 light field guns and 68 heavy guns. The Bolshevik plan was to overrun General Władysław Jędrzejewski's First Army with three field armies – the Fourth, Fifteenth and Third – with a force advantage of about 3:1.

The Polish defence followed the previous pattern, with a screen of strongpoints backed with reserves. The terrain in the area consisted of marshland and forest with several open corridors. The Polish 11th and 10th Infantry divisions were deployed in strongpoints along the Auta River, with a frontage of about 45km. Behind them and on either flank were the 8th Infantry Division on the Dysna River and the 17th Infantry Division on the main railway line to Minsk. Polish plans presumed that the response to a Bolshevik attack would be the commitment of reserves. However, the Kiev fighting had drained the area of reserves, most critically of cavalry.

In view of the Bolshevik advantages in resources, the results were predictable. The attack by the Bolshevik Fifteenth Army on 4 July pushed through the Polish strongpoints on the Auta River by the afternoon, and overcame the secondary defence lines by the following evening. The next defence line might have been the German trench line of 1917, except that its orientation left it exposed at its northern end, east of Wilno. By 11 July, the Bolshevik Fourth Army was well beyond the German trench line, facing a disorganized Polish First Army along the Wilja River on the approaches to Wilno. Gai's III Horse Corps, skirting along the Latvian–Lithuanian frontier, reached Święciany by 9 July. The Polish defences had resisted Bolshevik infantry attacks, but Gai's cavalry managed to find weak points along the river, capturing Wilno on 14 July and collapsing the northern wing of the Polish defences. During the Bolshevik operations in south-eastern

A Polish lancer (Ułan) regiment in the field during the 1920 campaign.

Lithuania, the Lithuanian government began negotiations with Moscow. In return for the transfer of Wilno to Lithuania, the Red Army was granted free passage through Lithuania, further undermining Polish defences on its northern shoulder.

With the collapse of the First Army in Belarus, the Polish army attempted to set up new defence lines further to the rear along the Nieman and Szczara rivers. The fortified city of Grodno was the anchor of the Polish defences on the left flank, but quickly came under attack by the 15th Cavalry Division on 19 July before the city's defences were adequately reinforced.

After being reinforced by the Bolshevik infantry of the Fourth Army, Gai's III Horse Corps continued westward past Grodno and over the Szczara River near Słonim. By 21 July, Polish attempts to re-establish defences over the Szczara had failed. Two days later, the Western Front made a broad assault over the Nieman. This forced the Polish First Army to withdraw to the Narew River. In less than three weeks of fighting, the Polish First Army retreated 400–500km. Most of the units retreated in good order, in part because Polish signals intelligence was able to keep track of Bolshevik units and steer the retreating Polish units away from traps. The Bolshevik Western Front moved inexorably forward, but the Red Army had a very limited appreciation of the location of the Polish dispositions and so was unable to encircle and destroy many large Polish formations.

POLITICAL REPERCUSSIONS

The Polish defeat in Ukraine led to a political crisis in Warsaw. Piłsudski was roundly criticized for the decision to proceed with the Kiev operation, which had been strongly opposed by Dmowski and the National Democrats. In an attempt to rein in Piłsudski and achieve a measure of national unity, a State Defence Council was created in Warsaw with representatives of the various parties. In the wake of the offensive in Belarus, the State Defence Council began arguing over the next course of action. Piłsudski offered to resign in order for the government to offer a more convincing peace plan, but the council rejected this suggestion. He urged the dispatch of a delegation to the conference of Entente leaders being held in early July in Spa, Belgium.

Premier Władysław Grabski reached Spa on 9 July, and acknowledged that Poland's predicament was in no small measure due to its own actions. Lloyd George criticized Poland's 'imperialistic and annexationist policy'. Britain proposed that the Polish army withdraw to the 8 December 1919 line in Belarus while remaining at the existing line in Galicia. He also demanded that Poland give up Wilno as a precondition to an armistice. The Polish delegation agreed to this. On 11 July, British foreign minister Lord George Curzon sent a note to Moscow proposing an armistice line, and warning that if Russia did not accept this, 'Great Britain and its Allies would be obliged to support the Polish nation with all means at its disposal'. Curzon suggested a border returning Belarus to Russia as well as ceding Russia the former Austrian province of eastern Galicia.

Poland's State Defence Council had mixed reactions to the Curzon note. The territorial concessions were greater than expected and placed several regions with significant Polish populations outside of the proposed borders. On the other hand, it suggested that the Entente would react militarily to a Russian incursion into Poland. Piłsudski was skeptical that Britain would actually provide troops to stem the Russian attack. While not rejecting the Curzon note, he also suggested that 'the war can be won, if the nation wants war'.

Moscow's reaction to the Curzon note was mixed. Some of the members, including Trotsky and foreign minister Chicherin, recommended accepting the note. Lenin took a far more adventurous position, feeling that the time was ripe to Sovietize Poland as the first step to igniting revolution in Germany and Europe. On 16 July, the Central Committee accepted Lenin's proposal that the primary missions be the liberation of 'the proletariat and toiling masses of Poland and Lithuania from their bourgeoisie and landlords'. For this to occur, the current offensive had to be strengthened. Although this remained the internal policy of the Bolshevik government, its public foreign policy was more moderate and conciliatory, and offered a guarantee of an independent Poland in a border further east than the Curzon line. This was subject to direct peace negotiations between Warsaw and Moscow, without involvement of the Entente.

Warsaw received the Bolshevik conditions on 20 July, and on 22 July, the foreign ministry offered an immediate armistice and opening of peace negotiations to Moscow. With the Red Army offensive proceeding rapidly, Moscow attempted to delay an armistice. Attempts by Poland to send a delegation to begin negotiations were deliberately frustrated by Moscow, prompting Britain to warn that a naval blockade would be started again and that arms would be provided to Poland. The Bolshevik peace negotiations were a charade disguising Lenin's revolutionary intent. The Central Committee on 5 August decided to continue the offensive until Poland was defeated; Glavkom Kamenev estimated that Warsaw would fall by 16 August. The Bolshevik delegation in London handed over armistice terms on 6 August under which Poland would be compelled to demilitarize and turn over the police functions to workers' militias, demands that were extreme enough to ensure their rejection.

Piłsudski's standing in Poland had suffered greatly as a result of the Polish army's rout. There was talk of replacing him as army chief, with the most likely candidate being Józef Dowbor-Muśnicki, who had strong support from Dmowski and the opposition National Democrats. To deflect some of the criticism, Piłsudski requested that General Tadeusz Rozwadowski take over as army chief of staff. Rozwadowski was well known and respected by the Entente, having been with the Polish delegation at the Versailles peace negotiations. He took over many of the day-to-day responsibilities for managing the army, allowing Piłsudski to concentrate on operational planning.

The Entente was disenchanted with Piłsudski's leadership. When General Maxime Weygand was sent to Poland as part of the Inter-Allied Military

The members of the Interallied Military Mission to Poland in Warsaw on 28 July 1920. In the second row is the head of the French delegation, General Maxime Weygand, whose role in the defence of Warsaw was controversial. To the left of Weygand in the British uniform is Maurice Hankey, representing British Prime Minister David Lloyd George. In the front row on the far left is Lord Edgar Vincent d'Abernon, British ambassador to Berlin and author of a famous book on the Battle of Warsaw.

The Polish army sponsored a Volunteers' Army Day in Warsaw in July 1920 to spur recruitment. Recruits of the Independent Workers' Association paraded with scythes, a patriotic gesture recalling the scythe-armed troops of the Kościuszko Rebellion of 1794.

Mission, there was some expectation that he would become the leader of the Polish army, in practice if not in title. He was disabused of this notion by Piłsudski. When they first met on 24 July, he was bluntly asked: 'How many divisions do you bring?' Weygand quickly realized that he had no appreciation for the details of the conflict, the combatants or the terrain. To avoid any embarrassment, he became advisor to Rozwadowski.

Piłsudski began planning a response to the Bolshevik invasion in late July. He believed that credit for the Bolshevik success in Ukraine had been largely due to Budënniy's First Horse Army, so a defeat of Budënniy's cavalry was essential to restoring the situation in the south-east. His solution was to create a Mounted Operational Group (*Grupa Operacyny Jazdy*) near Zamość under the command of General Jan Sawicki early in July 1920. To bolster the army, a campaign was begun to expand its forces through increased conscription and enlistments. A new Volunteer Army was created under General Haller as the centrepiece of this effort. Haller also was appointed to command the Northern Front in place of General Szeptycki, who was both ill and demoralized.

As the threat of a Russian invasion increased, patriotic sentiment in Poland stiffened. The Catholic Church, shocked by the widespread murder of village priests by the Bolsheviks as 'class enemies', bolstered the war effort from the pulpits. The Polish peasantry had not been enthusiastic about the war, but the Church's ardent support, and new legislation for land reform, gradually eroded their indifference. The head of the Peasant Party, Wincenty Witoś, was recruited by Piłsudski to lead a new government of national unity.

Piłsudski's strategic vision had long centred around his concept of the 'great combination' (*wielka kombinacja*), which referred to the use of Polesie as the Polish army's fulcrum of power. By controlling the rail lines through Polesie, the Polish army could shift its forces to either Belarus or Ukraine as the situation demanded. In the context of July 1920, Piłsudski wanted the Northern Front to buy time by delaying Tukhachevskiy's forces as long as possible to build up a counter-attack force. This Strike Force would be based slightly to the west of the Polesie area around Brest, and would attack northwards into Tukhachevskiy's left flank as it approached Warsaw.

The Red Army advance on Warsaw, 4 July–12 August 1920

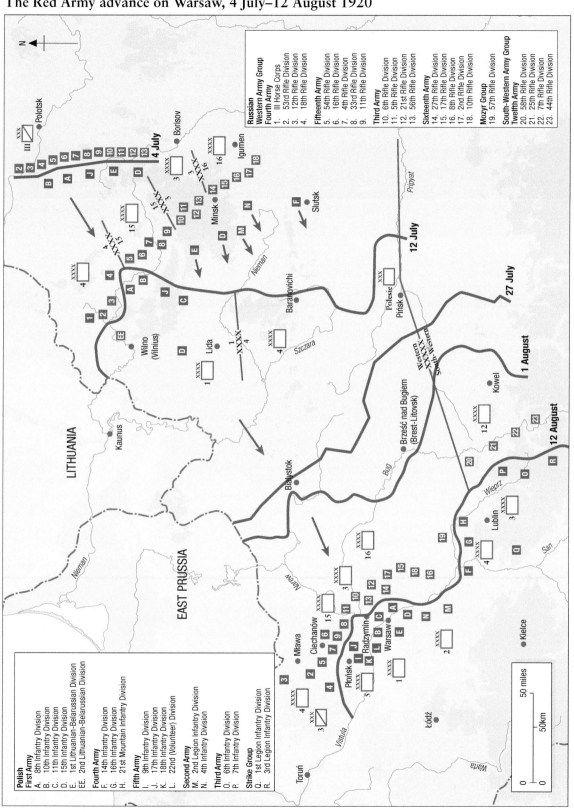

The offensive orientation of Piłsudski's solution was due to the Polish experiences during the previous year of fighting. Given the small size of forces available, defensive alignments could never be dense enough to repel a major attack. Offensive tactics had generally proved to be more successful, since neither side could concentrate the volume of firepower to resist attacks. Furthermore, the low level of training of soldiers on both sides, combined with the threadbare logistics, usually precipitated a rout once defensive lines were penetrated. Offence trumped defence in the east.

Piłsudski's plan was briefed to the French Military Mission by Rozwadowski on 27 July. The mission head, General Paul Henrys, strongly disagreed with the concept. He argued that the plan should focus entirely on a single counter-offensive blow, emanating from the Narew River against the Bolshevik Western Front. The Southern Front should be stripped of forces to reinforce the Northern Front, even if it meant abandoning Lwów. Rozwadowski indicated that a surrender of Lwów was unthinkable due to the political repercussions this would have in Poland. As a result, Henrys 'washed his hands' of the plan and warned the Poles that it would be entirely on their shoulders.

The plan continued to develop into early August. Piłsudski favoured a deep envelopment of Tukhachevskiy's Western Front. Piłsudski's plan to use Brest as the base for the counter-attack force was frustrated at the beginning of August when the Mozyr Group and elements of Sollogub's Sixteenth Army captured the fortress city during a battle there between 31 July and 2 August against General Sikorski's Polesie Group. This was a key point on the Polish line of defence along the Bug River, and the success of this attack opened the gate to Warsaw for Sollogub's Sixteenth Army over the course of the next week. A second bridgehead over the Bug was secured further north on the boundary between the Sixteenth Army and the Third Army to the north near Drohiczyn on 4 August 1920.

When Brest was lost on 2 August, Piłsudski changed the base of operations to the Wieprz River, well to the south-east of Warsaw, so that the counter-attack would not become entangled in the defence of Warsaw. Piłsudski envisioned this as a decisive battle that would determine the outcome of the conflict, not simply a campaign to halt the Bolshevik offensive. When Weygand arrived from France, he suggested a far less ambitious plan, emanating from the left wing of the Warsaw bridgehead, aimed primarily at cutting off the Bolshevik Fourth Army in western Poland. Rozwadowski's plan, like Piłsudski's, envisioned an attack out of the right flank of the Warsaw bridgehead, but with far less ambitious goals than Piłsudski's. In the event, it was Piłsudski's plan that would eventually take place. The orders for the counter-attack were issued on 6 August 1920. However, the forward advance of Tukhachevskiy's Western Front had to be stopped short of Warsaw for the plan to succeed.

SLOWING THE BOLSHEVIK ADVANCE

Although Tukhachevskiy's Western Front garnered most of the attention, Yegorev's South-Western Front continued to advance towards southern Poland. Piłsudski was far happier with the performance of Śmigły-Rydz's forces in Ukraine than Szeptycki's in Belarus. They had retreated in good order, and repeatedly counter-attacked with good effect. In early August,

Budënniy was halted for the first time. The Poles intercepted many of the key messages outlining the plans of the Twelfth Army and First Horse Army, particularly the change in strategic direction from a link-up with the Western Front at Brest to a more southerly advance towards Lwów. Piłsudski viewed the defeat or enfeeblement of Budënniy's First Horse Army a prerequisite to his planned counter-offensive. As a result, General Śmigły-Rydz began a series of actions aimed at nibbling away the First Horse Army.

General Franciszek Krajowski's 18th Infantry Division of the Polish Sixth Army had been assigned to defend Dubno during the retreat. It attacked the flank of the First Horse Army, bringing the full wrath of Budënniy's cavalry against it. Even after being reinforced with infantry from the Yakir Group, Budënniy was unable to overwhelm Krajowski's forces during the battle for Dubno on 19 July. In the event, one of the Bolshevik cavalry divisions finally found a gap in the Polish defences, obliging Krajowski to withdraw to the south-west. On 22 July, Krajowski and neighbouring units from the Polish Second Army further north attempted to cut off Budënniy again. The First Horse Army continued its advance towards Brody in spite of the flank attacks. By 1 August, the Poles had concentrated three infantry divisions around the First Horse Army in the vicinity of Brody. Sawicki's newly formed Mounted Operational Group was sent southwards to trap and finally destroy Budënniy. This effort was short-lived after Sawicki was ordered back north late on 1 August after the Bolshevik Sixteenth Army had attacked the key Polish defences at Brest. This reprieve allowed Budënniy to escape the trap at Brody. Although Piłsudski's plan to trap and destroy Budënniy had failed, the fighting for Brody and Dubno had severely weakened the First Horse Army and forced Yegorev to allow it to rest and recover for several days.

The first setbacks for Tukhachevskiy's Western Front came with their encounter with Żeligowski's Operational Group east of the Narew River in the Ostrołęka–Łomża–Ostrów triangle starting on 28 July. After nearly a month of rapid advances, the Red Army was finally beginning to run out of steam. A Polish parish priest described a Bolshevik rifle regiment passing through his village: 'the infantry … inspired pity, since most of the men were barefoot. Some wore civilian clothes, others the uniforms of various armies, mostly Polish ones, presumably from stores left behind by us in Belarus or

The 22nd Siedlice Infantry Regiment on the march in the summer of 1920. This unit was part of the 9th Infantry Division during the fighting in Ukraine in the summer of 1920 and was best known for its defence of Rechytsa on the Dnieper on 12 June 1920.

taken from prisoners. One's heart ached at the sight of this famished and tattered mob.'

Kork's Fifteenth Army and Lazarevich's Third Army finally overwhelmed the Polish defences along the Narew River on 2 August. Warsaw was soon in sight. By 11 August, the Sixteenth Army was approaching the main Warsaw bridgehead defences; the neighbouring Third Army advanced on Warsaw from the north-east.

Piłsudski had planned to launch his counter-attack in early August, but these intentions were frustrated by several factors. The loss of the staging area of Brest on 2 August disrupted the formation and deployment of Śmigły-Rydz's Strike Group. Furthermore, the attempts to crush Budënniy's cavalry in Galicia had been only partly successful. In addition, Polish signals intelligence had picked up a significant concentration of Bolshevik radio stations north of Polesie, which were first assessed to be a new Reserve Army arriving to reinforce the Western Front. This situation was not clarified until 3 August, when it became apparent that the radio stations were not from a phantom Reserve Army, but from the baggage trains of the Third Army that had become trapped far to the rear by the rapid pace of the Bolshevik advance.

On the eve of the battle for Warsaw, the Polish army consisted of three fronts. General Józef Haller's Northern Front consisted of three field armies. General Władysław Sikorski's Fifth Army, based around the fortress city of Modlin, shielded Warsaw to the north-east. General Franciszek Latinik's First Army defended Warsaw itself and General Bolesław Roja's Second Army was south of the capital. Piłsudski took direct command of the Central Front, south of the capital, which contained Śmigły-Rydz's Strike Group as well as General Leonard Skierski's Fourth Army and General Zygmunt Zieliński's Third Army. General Wacław Iwaszkiewicz's Southern Front in Galicia was the smallest of the three fronts, based around General Władysław Jędrzejewski's Sixth Army, with several separate infantry divisions, including the units of the Ukrainian army.

FUMBLING THE ENDGAME

On 15 July, Glavkom Kamenev offered Trotsky and Lenin a relatively sombre assessment of future prospects. He pointed out that even though the Red Army could conquer Poland, it would be exhausted and defending an extended line, in much the same predicament as Denikin's Volunteer Army the previous autumn. He also expressed concern over the threat posed by Romanian intervention into southern Ukraine near Odessa. Finally, Baron Wrangel's forces had used the Polish campaign as an opportunity to burst out of Crimea into the Tauride region, reopening the last major front of the Russian Civil War.

On 21 July, Kamenev visited Tukhachevskiy's new headquarters in Minsk. After consulting with Tukhachevskiy, Kamenev's caution evaporated and he became bolder in his assessment. On 23 July, he informed Trotsky that there was 'a feeling of great enthusiasm in the units that ensures the possibility of advancing further without lessening the speed'. He predicted that the war would be over in three weeks. This euphoria was contagious, and Lenin became more adventurous in his war aims. At the Second Congress of the Communist International in Petrograd, Lenin gloated that the Versailles

Expecting an imminent victory in Warsaw, in August 1920, Moscow set up the PolRevKom, a provisional puppet government for Poland, in the rectory of Wyszków, north-east of Warsaw. The two key members are seated in the second row: the de facto leader Feliks Dzierżyński, head of the Russian VCheKa secret police (second from the left), and chairman Julian Marchlewski (third from the left).

treaty would soon be extinguished. In a telegram to Stalin on 23 July, Lenin spoke about going beyond Poland to ignite revolution in Western Europe. The progress of Tukhachevskiy's Western Front had been so rapid, 600km in six weeks, that the advance towards Warsaw seemed an unstoppable avalanche.

These views affected Red Army planning for the final campaign within Poland. Kamenev's 21 July report suggested that Warsaw could be taken even if only three of the seven field armies operating in Poland were committed to this mission. Ivan Smilga, the RVSR representative to the Western Front, estimated that the Red Army would enjoy a 3:2 force ratio when arriving in the Warsaw area.

Instead of using the Fourth Army with its III Cavalry Corps to encircle Warsaw, it was dispatched into western Poland. This decision, advocated by Tukhachevskiy, was inspired by Lenin's dream that Germany was ripe for revolt. A French observer remarked that its mission was not so much fighting the Polish army as 'fighting the Treaty of Versailles'.

Shaposhnikov's original Vistula plan expected that the Western and South-Western fronts would join together at Brest, putting seven field armies in the decisive battle against the Polish army around Warsaw. Instead of directing Budënniy's First Horse Army to the north-west to reach Brest-Litovsk, on 23 July Kamenev instructed Yegorev to send Budënniy south-west to Lwów to crush the Polish resistance in Galicia. This decision was not shaped by local tactical issues so much as broader strategic concerns. The presence of the First Horse Army in Lwów would act as a counter-measure should Romania decide to intervene and cross the Dniester River into Ukraine. Furthermore, Lenin had pointed out to Stalin that the southern orientation of the South-Western Front would enable it to intervene should revolution break out again in Hungary as had occurred in 1919, perhaps spreading elsewhere in central Europe, including Czechoslovakia and Austria. At the time, Kamenev felt comfortable in not unifying the Western and South-Western fronts for the final drive on Warsaw, since Tukhachevskiy was extremely confident that his forces could do so without the aid of Yegorev's troops.

Another factor confusing Bolshevik decision-making was the distraction posed by Wrangel's operations from Crimea. Yegorev's South-Western Front controlled not only the three armies in Galicia, but the Thirteenth Army fighting Wrangel. On 31 July, Kamenev discussed a plan to shift three cavalry divisions and an infantry division from Budënniy to the Crimean Front. This was not expected to happen immediately, but in a few weeks after the Polish campaign was won. On 2 August, the Politburo decided that a new Southern Front would be created to deal with Wrangel, with Yegorev and Stalin earmarked as possible leaders there. At the same time, they decided to merge the Polish theatre into a single command under Tukhachevskiy. On 3 August, Kamenev instructed Yegorev to start establishing communication links between Budënniy's First Horse Army and the Twelfth Army with Tukhachevskiy's headquarters in Minsk as a prelude to unification of the Polish theatre. As will be related later, the instructions to change the command structure in the midst of major battles would end in confusion and acrimony.

The serious misjudgements about the situation on the Polish front were partly due to poor intelligence assessments. The Russians had relatively good tactical intelligence about Polish forces facing them by using traditional methods such as POW interrogations. However, with little aerial reconnaissance and no signals intelligence, the Red Army had a very poor appreciation of the strategic situation of the Polish army in terms of its reserves and intentions. The rapid defeat of Polish forces in June and July 1920 led to the assumption that the Polish army was weaker than it actually was, and that it was on the verge of defeat.

There might have been some hint of the resilience of the Polish army by a more sober assessment of the scale of prisoners taken between May and July. Only about 25,000 prisoners had been taken, and only about 40 field guns seized. These numbers were significant but they did not represent the capture of any large Polish formations. The Polish army had been successful in replacing its losses suffered from January through to August 1920 with 164,615 new recruits versus total casualties of 150,900.

BATTLES ALONG THE WARSAW BRIDGEHEAD

The first Bolshevik formations began arriving at the Warsaw Bridgehead on the evening of 12 August, starting in the Third Army's sector north-east of the city. Through the next morning, five rifle divisions of Sollogub's Sixteenth Army arrived along a broad front opposite Warsaw. Heavy fighting broke out on the morning of 13 August all along the perimeter. The Red Army had its greatest success in the northern sector on the boundary of the Third and Sixteenth armies when the 21st Rifle Division (Third Army) and 27th Rifle Division (Sixteenth Army) pushed through the Polish 11th Division defences around the town of Radzymin.

Polish signals intelligence intercepted and decrypted Sollogub's instructions to his rifle divisions in the Radzymin sector for the following day's operation. Recognizing the Radzymin area as key to the Bolshevik plans, Haller mobilized two of his reserve divisions, the 1st Lithuanian-Belarussian Division and the 10th Division, and sent them to reinforce the 11th Infantry Division.

The fighting on the Warsaw Bridgehead was fundamentally unlike the previous campaign. The Poles had created elaborate trench defences and this was the only time in the campaign that the density of opposing forces approached World War I levels. It was one of the few times when Polish tanks were used in significant numbers.

The fighting on 14 August saw further penetrations of the Polish defences beyond Radzymin by the same two rifle divisions. Tukhachevskiy was unable to quickly reinforce this sector, lacking adequate reserves. By this stage, Sollogub's Sixteenth Army was down to only about 21,000 combatants facing Polish forces numbering about 38,000 behind stout defences.

The citizens of Warsaw turn out at the railway station to wave farewell to Polish troops going to the front in August 1920. Railways were the principal means of military transport in the 1919–20 campaigns due to the lack of roads and motor transport in the Borderlands.

On 14 August, the Polish 11th Division attempted to stem the Radzymin penetration by counter-attacks on both flanks, reinforced by regiments of the 1st Lithuanian-Belarussian Division. The arrival of the reinforcements on 14 and 15 August turned the tide of the battle, pinching off the Bolshevik penetration from both flanks. The town of Radzymin changed hands five times during the three-day battle. Sollogub's Sixteenth Army had very little success in other sectors of the Warsaw Bridgehead, managing some local penetrations that were quickly staunched by the Poles.

Sikorski's Fifth Army, north of Warsaw, had only deployed on 10 August and had a meagre 22,000 bayonets and 4,000 sabres. Its composition was unusually varied, even by Polish standards. Among its formations was Krajowski's understrength but battle-hardened 18th Infantry Division, transferred to the Modlin area for rebuilding after its combat with Budënniy the previous month. Another of its formations was the 22nd (Volunteer) Division, made up of an assortment of students, artists and priests, hastily inducted and trained. An equally unusual formation was the Siberian Brigade, formed from Polish conscripts of the old Russian army, re-equipped in Vladivostok with American and Japanese small arms, and dispatched on a six-month sea voyage back to Poland. When initially deployed, it still lacked its rifles.

Opposite Sikorski's Fifth Army were three Bolshevik field armies: from north to south, the Fourth, Fifteenth and Third armies, with a total of about 74,000 combatants. The Fourth Army was racing westwards towards the German frontier and did not make extensive contact with Sikorski's forces. Avgust Kork's Fifteenth Army was beginning a wheeling motion, attempting to approach Warsaw from behind. The Bolshevik force most heavily in contact with Sikorski was the Third Army, stretched from the northern approaches of Warsaw and already partly engaged with the Polish First Army.

Rather than wait for the Bolsheviks to get their troops into position, Haller instructed Sikorski to speed up his plans and to advance over the Wkra and

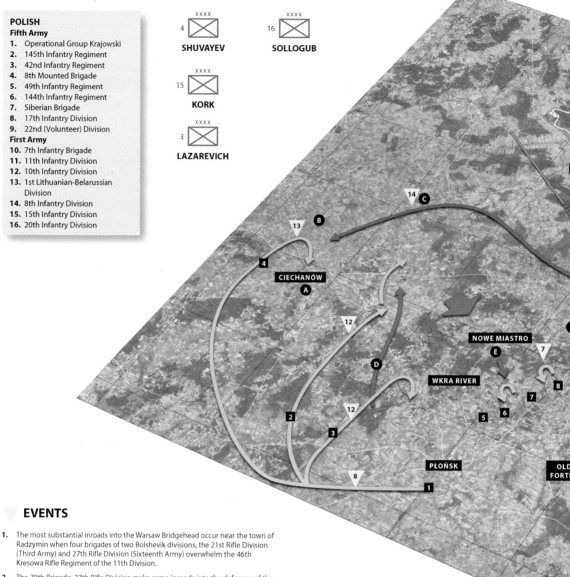

POLISH

Fifth Army
1. Operational Group Krajowski
2. 145th Infantry Regiment
3. 42nd Infantry Regiment
4. 8th Mounted Brigade
5. 49th Infantry Regiment
6. 144th Infantry Regiment
7. Siberian Brigade
8. 17th Infantry Division
9. 22nd (Volunteer) Division

First Army
10. 7th Infantry Brigade
11. 11th Infantry Division
12. 10th Infantry Division
13. 1st Lithuanian-Belarussian Division
14. 8th Infantry Division
15. 15th Infantry Division
16. 20th Infantry Division

SHUVAYEV 4

SOLLOGUB 16

KORK 15

LAZAREVICH 3

CIECHANÓW

NOWE MIASTRO

WKRA RIVER

PŁOŃSK

OLD FORTI

EVENTS

1. The most substantial inroads into the Warsaw Bridgehead occur near the town of Radzymin when four brigades of two Bolshevik divisions, the 21st Rifle Division (Third Army) and 27th Rifle Division (Sixteenth Army) overwhelm the 46th Kresowa Rifle Regiment of the 11th Division.

2. The 79th Brigade, 27th Rifle Division make some inroads into the defences of the 47th Kresowa Rifles, 11th Infantry Division, before being pushed back by Polish counter-attacks.

3. Haller mobilizes two of his reserve divisions, the 1st Lithuanian-Belarussian Division and the 10th Division, and sends them to reinforce the 11th Infantry Division around Radzymin.

4. The 7th Infantry Brigade, covering the city defences north of the Narew River, holds back attacks by the Bolshevik 6th Rifle Division on 13–15 August.

5. Radzymin remains the main focus of the fighting on 14 August, with regiments of the 21st Rifle Division making the deepest penetrations of the Polish defences beyond Radzymin. The northern shoulder is held by the 48th Kresowa Rifle Regiment. The southern shoulder of the penetration is counter-attacked by elements of the 46th and 47th Kresowa Rifles, with initial reinforcements arriving from the 1st Lithuanian-Belarussian Division.

6. The 79th Brigade of the 27th Rifle Division penetrates the Polish defence line at the boundary between the 8th and 11th Infantry divisions, but is halted by Polish counter-attacks.

7. On 14 August, hasty Polish attacks across the Wkra River by the Siberian Brigade, Volunteer Division and assorted infantry regiments against the 11th and 16th Rifle divisions of the Fifteenth Army are thrown back.

8. On 14 August, General Franciszek Krajowski of the 18th Infantry Division leads an improvised operational group consisting of the 42nd and 145th Infantry regiments and Colonel Karnicki's 8th Cavalry Brigade. They pass through a gap between the Bolshevik Fourth and Fifteenth armies, making limited contact.

9. The decisive fighting for Radzymin takes place on 15 August when elements of the Polish 10th and 11th Infantry divisions strike the Bolshevik salient from the north while the 1st Lithuanian-Belarussian Division attacks from the south, eventually pinching off the penetration. The town of Radzymin changes hands five times during the two-day battle.

10. Attacks by the 10th Rifle Division against the 15th Infantry Division fail to make any inroads into the Polish defences.

11. Renewed attacks by the 79th Brigade, 27th Rifle Division against the 47th Kresowa Regiment are pushed back on 15 August.

12. On 15 August, the 42nd and 145th Infantry regiments outflank the Bolshevik 4th Rifle Division, forcing it to withdraw. Krajowski's armoured car detachment stages a raid into the rear of the 18th Rifle Division, Fourth Army, west of Płońsk, engaging in a two-hour battle with two of its regiments.

13. The 8th Cavalry Brigade arrives outside Ciechanów on the evening of 14 August; its 203rd Lancers enter the town on the morning of 15 August. Komarm A. D. Shuvayev's Fourth Army headquarters is overrun, with Shuvayev fleeing to Mława and his staff to Ostrołęka.

14. The raiding by Krajowski's group forces the Fifteenth Army to shift two of its rifle divisions back towards Ciechanów to deal with the threat to the army's rear area.

THE BATTLE FOR WARSAW, 13–15 AUGUST 1920

On the eve of the battle for the city, Sikorski's Fifth Army was based around the fortress city of Modlin, shielding Warsaw to the north-east. Latinik's First Army defended Warsaw itself, with Roja's Second Army south of the capital.

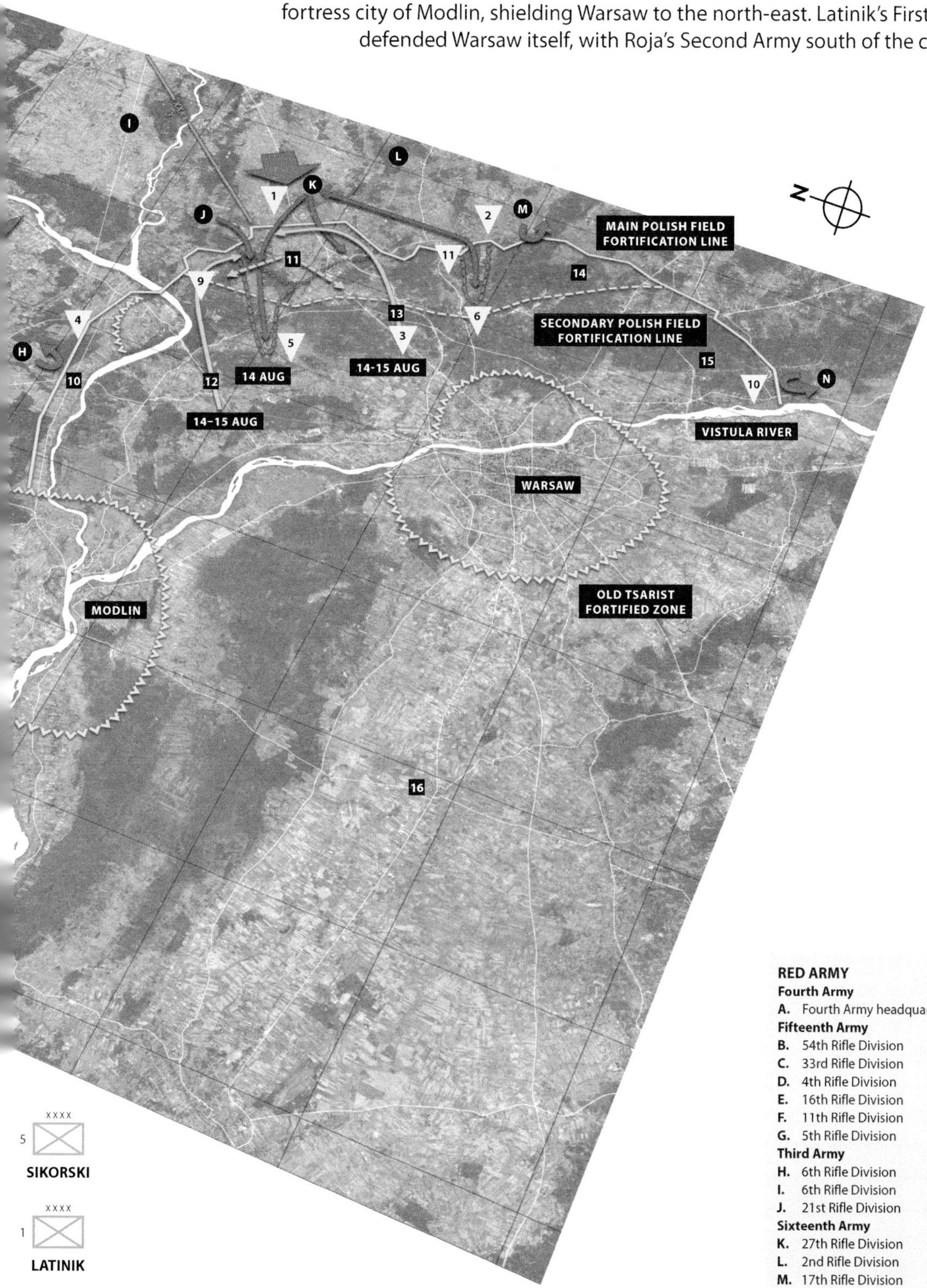

N
MAIN POLISH FIELD FORTIFICATION LINE
SECONDARY POLISH FIELD FORTIFICATION LINE
14 AUG
14-15 AUG
14-15 AUG
VISTULA RIVER
WARSAW
MODLIN
OLD TSARIST FORTIFIED ZONE
I
J
K
L
M
H
N
1
2
3
4
5
6
9
10
10
11
11
12
13
14
15
16

XXXX
5 SIKORSKI

XXXX
1 LATINIK

RED ARMY

Fourth Army

A. Fourth Army headquarters

Fifteenth Army

B. 54th Rifle Division
C. 33rd Rifle Division
D. 4th Rifle Division
E. 16th Rifle Division
F. 11th Rifle Division
G. 5th Rifle Division

Third Army

H. 6th Rifle Division
I. 6th Rifle Division
J. 21st Rifle Division

Sixteenth Army

K. 27th Rifle Division
L. 2nd Rifle Division
M. 17th Rifle Division
N. 10th Rifle Division

Note: gridlines are shown at intervals of 20km (12.43 miles)

A 122mm howitzer M1909 of the Red Army's 8th Rifle Division, Sixteenth Army, during the fighting west of the Bug River in the summer of 1920. This was the standard Russian heavy divisional cannon.

Vistula rivers a day early on 14 August while Bolshevik forces were still in transit. Sikorski reminded Haller that he was commanding an army in name only, since many of his forces had not yet arrived or lacked their weapons. The initial attacks over the Wkra River against the 11th and 16th Rifle divisions of the Fifteenth Army were thrown back. Sikorski was able to shield the defences along the Wkra River with aggressive patrolling by his two armoured trains that served as roving artillery over the next several days.

In view of the gross disparity in forces between his Fifth Army and the three field armies of the Western Front, Sikorski decided that his best solution was to try to disrupt the Bolshevik forces by aggressive tactics. General Franciszek Krajowski of the 18th Infantry Division led an improvised group consisting of two infantry regiments and Karnicki's 8th Cavalry Brigade. Karnicki's brigade included a detachment of eight Ford Model T armoured cars, each armed with a machine gun.

The 42nd and 145th Infantry regiments outflanked the Bolshevik 4th Rifle Division, forcing it to withdraw. The armoured car detachment staged a raid into the rear of the 18th Rifle Division, Fourth Army, west of Płońsk, engaging in a two-hour battle with two of its regiments. In the meantime, the 8th Cavalry Brigade began a deep raid against the rear areas of the Fourth Army near Ciechanów.

By the time of the Battle of Warsaw, the Polish army deployed 79 armoured cars, most of them captured Russian types. This is a Russkiy-Ostin originally called *Stenka Razin* in Bolshevik service with the 1st Armoured Car Detachment and renamed *Poznańczyk* after its capture on 28 May 1920 by the 55th Poznań Infantry Regiment, during the fighting near Bobruisk. In front are Captain Edward Korwin-Kossakowski and Lieutenant Witold Orłowski.

Komarm Aleksandr D. Shuvayev's Fourth Army headquarters was temporarily camped in Ciechanów when the Polish cavalry arrived unexpectedly on the morning of 15 August. Shuvayev ordered the headquarters' equipment to be demolished or burned. As a result, the Fourth Army lost its radio stations, its only means to communicate with Tukhachevskiy's Western Front headquarters. Furthermore, Karnicki's cavalry captured much of the headquarters' papers, including plans and cypher books. The attacks by Sikorski's Fifth Army seized the initiative in this sector and forced the Bolshevik Third and Fifteenth armies to delay the planned encirclement of Warsaw. By the evening of 15 August, both the Third and Fifteenth armies were running out of artillery ammunition and other supplies, further impeding their advance.

The Western Front tried to crush Sikorski's Fifth Army on 16 August with fresh attacks by Lazarevich's Third Army near Nasielsk. By this stage, Haller had finally appreciated the severity of the threat against Sikorski's small army, and during the afternoon of 16 August, reinforcements arrived, temporarily stabilizing the front. This was the most vulnerable sector of the Warsaw front, yet Tukhachevskiy failed to concentrate his forces to overwhelm it. Part of the problem was the loss of communication with the Fourth Army, but both the Third and Fifteenth armies still had substantial resources in this area totaling nine divisions. The main problem was that the Red Army was exhausted, and short of ammunition and supplies.

General Władysław Sikorski, commander of the Polish Fifth Army that defended the northern flank of Warsaw in August 1920. In World War II, Sikorski led the Polish government in exile in Britain until his death in 1943 in an airplane accident.

Sikorski's Fifth Army had a small armoured car detachment equipped with Ford Model T automobiles converted into small armoured cars. This is a recent reconstruction of one of the Ford armoured cars. (Wojciech Łuczak)

PIŁSUDSKI'S COUNTER-ATTACK

Piłsudski issued the orders for the counter-offensive on 6 August, and left Warsaw to take personal command of the Central Front on 12 August. There was some anxiety in the Polish high command after signals intelligence intercepted a 7 August message from Tukhachevskiy to Glavkom Kamenev regarding the assignment of the First Horse Army and Twelfth Army to the Western Front. If these forces moved into the Lublin Gap, they might trap Śmigły-Rydz's Strike Group before it acted. In the event, the intelligence evidence over the next few days showed these forces were tied down in the fighting around Lwów, and not moving towards Lublin. Curiously enough, Tukhachevskiy received a copy of Piłsudski's plan from the body of a dead Polish officer near Chełm. He discussed this with Kamenev on 13 August, but dismissed it as a deception.

The failure of Yegorev's headquarters to transfer the Twelfth Army and the First Horse Army to assist in the Battle

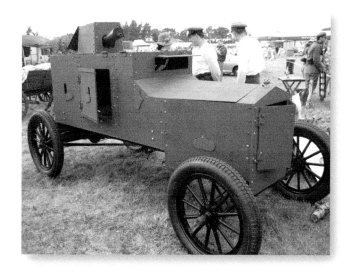

Piłsudski's counter-attack, 16–25 August 1920

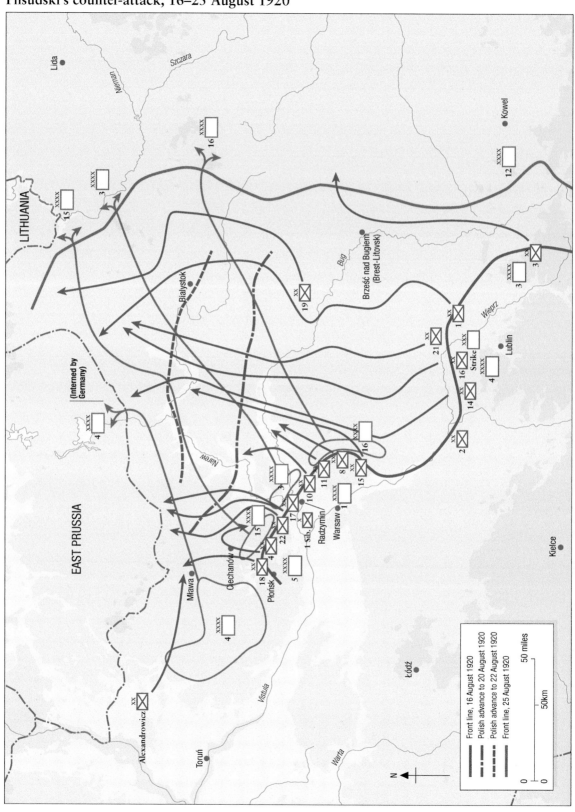

of Warsaw would become one of the greatest controversies of the war. There already was bad blood between Tukhachevskiy and Yegorev over Tukhachevskiy's earlier refusal to transfer two divisions to the Thirteenth Army for the fight with Wrangel. As mentioned above, the debate over the allotment of the First Horse Army had been festering since earlier in August. On 7 August, Tukhachevskiy sent a telegram to Kamenev declining to take control of the Twelfth Army and First Horse Army unless several conditions were met. Yegorev and Stalin replied that those conditions would dismantle their headquarters prior to its transfer to the Crimea to deal with Wrangel.

On top of this discord, Kamenev began to worry that Tukhachevskiy had underestimated the threat immediately south-east of Warsaw around Lublin. Tukhachevskiy's plan had been to concentrate his attack on Warsaw from the north-east rather than directly from the east. On 11 August, Kamenev explained these concerns to Tukhachevskiy, suggesting that the Warsaw attack also be conducted over the Bug from east of the city.

Later in the day, Kamenev ordered the transfer of the Twelfth Army to the Western Front on 13 August, and the First Horse Army on 15 August, but he couched the instructions in equivocal terms, asking for Yegorev's opinion on the transfer. Was this an order or a proposal? That same day, Stalin received a telegram from Lenin emphasizing the need to deal promptly with Wrangel, hinting that the South-Western Front had to retain enough power to carry out this forthcoming mission. Yegorev and Stalin did not reply to Kamenev's message until 13 August, blaming decipherment problems. They responded negatively to the transfer, stating that it was impossible, since both armies were engaged at Lwów. Kamenev responded with a firm order that both the Twelfth Army and First Horse Army would be transferred to the Western Front by noon on 14 August. Stalin refused to sign the order from the front headquarters to the field armies, and was recalled to Moscow to explain his actions.

With the spires of Lwów in sight, Budënniy and Voroshilov were annoyed on 16 August to receive another order transferring them immediately to Tukhachevskiy's command, disengaging from Lwów and redirecting them towards Lublin. The order lacked sufficient signatures from the RVSR representatives, and so Budënniy sent a telegram back to Tukhachevskiy noting that it was invalid. Tukhachevskiy sent back the orders twice more on

Polish infantry from the 15th Infantry Division advance in late August 1920 near Wiązowna during Piłsudski's counter-offensive. This unit fought against the Bolshevik Sixteenth Army during the Warsaw campaign.

Piłsudski converses with General Edward Śmigły-Rydz at his forward command post during the fighting along the Nieman River in September 1920.

17 and 19 August; by this time, Piłsudski's counter-offensive was underway. Voroshilov raised the matter directly with the RVSR on 20 August, only to be told the order was valid and to begin moving to Lublin. This disagreement delayed the transfer of the First Horse Army by a week, by which time it was irrelevant to the Battle of Warsaw.

Historians ever since have argued whether an early transfer of Budënniy's First Horse Army to Lublin might not have disrupted Piłsudski's counter-offensive. Even had the transfer taken place, it is far from certain that Budënniy could have derailed the Polish counter-offensive. The First Horse Army had suffered significant losses in early August and was entangled with the Polish Sixth Army. The transfer towards Lublin would have led to an attritional struggle along the route and so may not have had a significant impact on Piłsudski's attack. However, the political outcome of this controversy would have long-term and brutal consequences.

Piłsudski waited until Tukhachevskiy's Western Front was fully engaged with the Warsaw defences before finally signalling the start of the counter-offensive. Although planned for 17 August, he pushed it up a day to the morning of 16 August. Skierski's Fourth Army advanced northwards, striking the left flank of the Bolshevik Sixteenth Army. Śmigły-Rydz's Strike Group, consisting of the 1st and 3rd Legion divisions and two cavalry brigades, had the exploitation missions. They pushed deep behind the Western Front, well to the east of Warsaw. Zieliński's Third Army had two missions: an offensive strike towards Brest, and a defensive mission to the south to rebuff any advance of the Twelfth Army and First Horse Army from Galicia. The Polish forces numbered about 49,000 combatants.

Lieutenant-General Daniel Konarzewski's 14th Infantry Division overwhelmed the Bolshevik 57th Rifle Division on the left wing of the Sixteenth Army near the village of Cyców. The Strike Group dealt with Bolshevik units further to the rear with the 1st Legion Division overwhelming the Mozyr Group around Radzyń and the 3rd Legion Division attacking the 58th Rifle Division at Włodawa. The weak and overextended Mozyr Group, with only about 8,000 combatants, had been assigned to shield the Western Front from any Polish attacks from the south, and its disintegration exposed the entire left flank of Tukhachevskiy's forces.

In concert with Piłsudski's offensive, the Polish army disrupted Bolshevik command and control by jamming the Russian radio command net. By this stage, the Western Front was entirely dependent on radio communication, since it was far removed from secure telegraph lines. The Poles broadcast passages from the Gospel of St John on select radio command frequencies during the first critical days of the counter-offensive.

Yegorev was instructed to push the Twelfth Army northwards towards Hrubieszów to threaten the flank of the Polish counter-attack force, but these attacks were pushed back by Zieliński's Third Army. The Bolshevik Sixteenth Army, especially its left wing, was trapped between the advancing Polish Fourth Army behind them and the defending First Army in front of them, and began to crumble, especially in the south. During the first three days of the counter-offensive, the Poles captured 10,000 Bolshevik prisoners.

The Bolshevik Fourth Army was isolated along the Prussian frontier, unaware of Piłsudski's counter-offensive after the loss of its radio stations at Ciechanów. Its spearhead, Gai's III Horse Corps, was still racing westwards towards Toruń and the Pomeranian corridor. Using couriers, Tukhachevskiy ordered it to re-establish contact with the Fifteenth Army with another attempt to seize the town of Płońsk. The Fifteenth Army advanced on Płońsk from the north-east with two rifle divisions, while the Fourth Army attacked from the north-west of the city. Polish signals intelligence warned Sikorski's Fifth Army about this threat and an improvised battlegroup under Colonel Gustaw Orlicz-Dreszer rushed to the town to defend it. The battle for Płońsk was decided on 17 August. The Fifteenth Army attack was halted by the 18th Infantry Division south of Ciechanów. Orlicz-Dreszer's troops defended the town. At a critical point, the 1st Light Horse Regiment caught the 18th Rifle Division in the open, and the mounted attack forced the Bolshevik infantry to withdraw in disorder. The failure to secure Płońsk isolated the Fourth Army from the rest of the Western Front, leading to its eventual rout.

Tukhachevskiy's headquarters in Minsk lost communication with many of its field armies in the wake of the Polish counter-offensive, resulting in a stream of orders that had little basis in reality. In the absence of control from higher headquarters, and realizing they were being cut off from behind, the Bolshevik field armies began withdrawing haphazardly from the Warsaw Bridgehead on 17 and 18 August. Piłsudski instructed Latinik's First Army to begin pursuing the retreating Sixteenth Army, but in view of the precarious and chaotic situation to the north, Latinik reinforced Sikorski's Fifth Army in its continuing struggles with the three Bolshevik field armies still north of Warsaw.

The Bolshevik high command was largely unaware of the scale of the unfolding catastrophe. Sollogub's Sixteenth Army had already disintegrated and was in an uncontrolled retreat back towards Białystok. Gai's III Horse Corps had become detached from Shuvayev's Fourth Army in western Poland. In desperation, Tukhachevskiy issued instructions to Kork's Fifteenth Army and Lazarevich's Third Army to wheel around Warsaw from the north-east and enter Warsaw from its undefended western side. Given the weakness of both these armies and the growing strength of

POLISH
1st Mounted Division
1. 6th Mounted Brigade
2. 1st Lancers
3. 12th Lancers
4. 14th Lancers
5. 7th Mounted Brigade
6. 2nd Light Horse
7. 8th Lancers
8. 9th Lancers
9. 26th Infantry Brigade

XXXX
1
BUDËNNIY

MAJDAN WOODS

HILL

WOLICA ŚNIATYCKA

KOMARÓW

EVENTS

1. The 11th Cavalry Division sends one brigade south from the Majdan Woods to clear a path towards Komarów, but is stopped on encountering the 26th Infantry Brigade entrenched west of Wolica Śniatycka.

2. The 11th Cavalry Division's other brigade heads out of the Majdan Woods for Wolica Śniatycka, encountering the forward elements of the Polish 7th Cavalry Brigade on Hill 255.

3. The 2nd Light Horse Regiment charges the Bolshevik brigade, but is forced to retreat back to Hill 255.

4. The 9th Lancers enter the mêlée, managing to push the Bolshevik brigade back northwards to Cześniki.

5. The Bolshevik Special Brigade joins the cavalry mêlée around 1000hrs, forcing the two Polish regiments back to Hill 255.

6. Captain Tadeusz Komorowski's 12th Podolian Lancers advance from Śniatycze and charge the right flank of the Separate Cavalry Brigade before it reaches Hill 255.

7. Two regiments of the 6th Cavalry Brigade appear south of Komarów, convincing Komdiv F. M. Morozov to withdraw the 11th Cavalry Division back to the Cześniki area around noon, and bringing a temporary end to the fighting.

8. The 6th Mounted Brigade passes through the Komarów area to the north-east; the 7th Mounted Brigade is instructed to follow later in the afternoon.

9. The Bolshevik 6th Cavalry Division, delayed in its attack by the late arrival of its 2nd Brigade, finally arrives in the Komarów area around 1800hrs. It catches the tail end of the 7th Mounted Brigade as it is moving north-east after the 6th Brigade.

10. The 9th Lancers charge the 6th Cavalry Division but are overrun. The 8th Lancers intervene, but are too weak to stop the 6th Cavalry Division.

11. The 1st Lancers, the trailing formation of the 6th Mounted Brigade, spot the cavalry mêlée and charge the Bolshevik cavalry. This mounted charge breaks the momentum of the 6th Cavalry Division attack, and the Red cavalry withdraws northwards to Cześniki.

BATTLE OF KOMARÓW, 31 AUGUST 1920

The First Horse Army is defeated at Komarów, and forced to retreat.
This is the last grand cavalry vs. cavalry battle in European history.

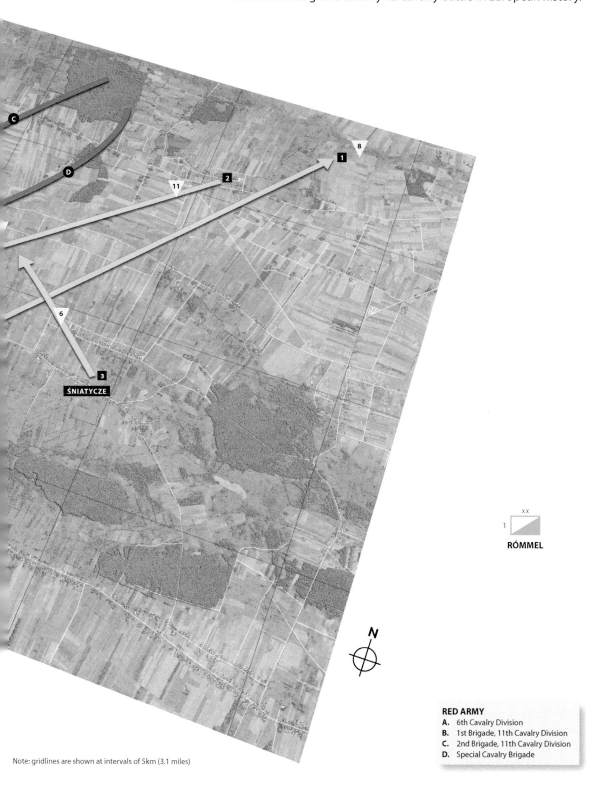

ŚNIATYCZE

RÓMMEL

N

RED ARMY
A. 6th Cavalry Division
B. 1st Brigade, 11th Cavalry Division
C. 2nd Brigade, 11th Cavalry Division
D. Special Cavalry Brigade

Note: gridlines are shown at intervals of 5km (3.1 miles)

Sikorski's Fifth Army, this was sheer fantasy. Tukhachevskiy did not fully comprehend the situation until 20 August, at which point he ordered a general retreat.

Gai's III Horse Corps, now trapped behind Polish lines, tried to escape eastwards. Sikorski's Fifth Army attempted to capture the remnants of Shuvayev's Fourth Army and Gai's cavalry, and a perimeter was established along the Mława–Ciechanów railway line. On 22 and 23 August, Gai's cavalry overran Polish detachments trying to block their escape. They were finally blocked by the 14th Infantry Division on 26 August near Kolno. Expecting no mercy from the Poles due to a string of massacres against Polish civilians and prisoners of war, Gai decided to seek internment in Germany instead of surrender. Nearly all of Gai's cavalry along with the rest of Shuvayev's Fourth Army ended up crossing the border into East Prussia, eventually totalling 65,000–90,000 Bolshevik troops.

THE BATTLE OF THE ZAMOŚĆ RING

The fighting to the north-east of Warsaw largely ended by late August, except for skirmishes between Polish patrols and Bolshevik stragglers still trying to escape. However, fighting still continued in Galicia. By the time that the First Horse Army and Twelfth Army had disengaged from the fighting at Lwów, the mission to reinforce the Warsaw attack had become pointless. Nonetheless, Kamenev felt that a raid towards Lublin would distract the Polish army while some semblance of order could be restored on the Western Front.

In the meantime, Władysław Sikorski had been transferred from command of the Fifth Army north of Warsaw to the Third Army along the Bug River with the specific mission of finally crushing Budёnniy's cavalry and pushing the Bolsheviks out of Galicia. With the battle against the Western Front largely won, additional Polish divisions were sent to Galicia to assist in this mission.

After resting for several days, Budёnniy led the First Horse Army and the Twelfth Army towards Zamość. He reached the old fortified city on 29 August, but found that it was stoutly defended by the Polish 31st Infantry Regiment. Patrols had made him aware that Polish forces were closing in on all sides. He also finally learned from Polish prisoners that the Western Front had been routed near Warsaw and fled back to the Nieman River. At the time, his forces totalled 11,597 sabres, 1,418 bayonets, 387 machine guns and 72 field guns. On 30 August, he realized that he was trapped within a ring of Polish formations, but movement was made difficult by the recent summer rains that had left much of the area in deep mud.

To the north-west and north, Budёnniy was cut off by the approaching Third Army's two infantry divisions, to the south-west by Stanisław Haller's 13th Infantry Division. As a result, an escape southwards seemed the best option. While the 14th Cavalry Division patrolled the northern flank, and the 6th Cavalry Division along the south-western flank, Budёnniy moved south-eastwards on 31 August with the 4th and 11th Cavalry divisions and the Separate Cavalry Brigade, planning to escape by way of Komarów and Tyszowce.

Approaching Komarów from the south-east was Colonel Julius Rómmel's 1st Mounted Division. This force was less than a third of the size of

Budënniy's First Horse Army. On 31 August, the Polish cavalry clashed with the Red cavalry in the fields north of Komarów in the last grand cavalry vs. cavalry battle in European history. Although substantially outnumbered, the fresh Polish cavalry managed to repulse Budënniy's uncoordinated attacks. Casualties in the Polish 1st Mounted Division were about 300 men, roughly one-fifth of its starting strength, along with 500 horses. The elements of the First Horse Army that took part in the battle for Komarów had a starting strength of about 4,100 sabres, including 1,800 in the 6th Cavalry Division, 1,500 in the 11th Cavalry Division and 800 in the Special Brigade. These units lost about 1,500 killed during the battles around Komarów and they left behind most of the First Horse Army's war booty. Nevertheless, they managed to retreat to the Huczwa River and escape through the weak defences of the 2nd Legion Infantry Division. The Battle of the Zamość Ring broke the back of the First Horse Army and it played no significant role in the Polish theatre afterwards.

FINAL BATTLES

By the end of August, Tukhachevskiy's Western Front had lost about 170,000 men, consisting of about 25,000 killed, 66,000 captured by the Poles and 65,000–90,000 interned in Germany. On reaching the Nieman and Szczara rivers, it could muster only about 30,000 combatants. In view of the volatility of the previous campaigns, Tukhachevskiy believed that a fresh infusion of troops could give him enough strength to rebuff the Poles. The Red Army had moved up reserves of about 70,000 men at Vitebsk in the Smolensk Gate area, and he estimated that by late September, he could build the front back up to a quarter of a million men. In spite of the paper strength of the Western Front, its combat power had in fact been gutted. The campaign had destroyed its infrastructure and much of his force was completely demoralized.

A number of Kuban Cossack units joined the Polish Army in 1919 and 1920. This Cossack unit is seen on the march in 1920 along with some Polish officers of the 7th Lublin Lancer Regiment. The Cossack Independent Brigade fought during the Battle of the Zamość Ring in August 1920.

General Lucjan Żeligowski led the Polish venture to seize the Wilno area in September 1920, ostensibly without Warsaw's approval.

Piłsudski was determined to deny Tukhachevskiy any time to rebuild. On 21 September, Śmigły-Rudz's Second Army launched an assault over the Nieman River to take the city of Grodno from Lazerevich's Third Army. The city was well defended by fresh troops and the fighting was hard. Piłsudski then sent the 1st Legion Division and the 1st Lithuanian-Belarussian Division along with two cavalry brigades through Lithuanian territory, aiming to cut off the Grodno garrison from behind by taking the city of Lida to the east. On 25 September, Tukhachevskiy authorized Lazarevich to retreat; in fact, much of the Third Army had already fled. On the night of 25/26 September, the Polish divisions marched into Grodno.

The situation for the Red Army in the sectors further south was even worse. Shuvayev and his staff were all that remained of the original Fourth Army, and in September, a new field army was hastily created around this kernel to defend Polesie. Krajowski's 18th Infantry Division and Stanisław Bułak-Bałachowicz's Belarussian Volunteer Army seized Pinsk. The Bolshevik 17th Cavalry Division defected to Bułak-Bałachowicz, and the stillborn Fourth Army disintegrated.

At the Ninth All-Russian Conference of the Bolshevik Party in September 1920, Lenin acknowledged that the Red Army was exhausted and reluctant to continue the war. On 20 September, the Central Committee created a special commission to draft conditions for a peace treaty. The initial border proposal offered by Moscow was immediately to the east of the Curzon Line, which was unacceptable to Warsaw. On 5 October 1920, a tentative agreement was reached in Riga after Bolshevik territorial concessions were offered.

The indecisive results of the initial peace negotiations encouraged the Polish army to continue to push eastwards. On 28 September, Tukhachevskiy authorized a general retreat to the German 1917 trench line. Attempts to re-establish a coherent defence line failed, and the Polish army continued to advance on a broad front, aiming to seize as much territory as possible to use as leverage in the negotiations.

A remaining controversy was the fate of Wilno. Moscow had ceded Wilno to Lithuania as a result of its July treaty and turned over control on 26 August. The Poles had renounced Wilno in their agreement with the Entente at Spa earlier in the summer, and the government was not anxious to extend the war into Lithuania. However, Lithuania had granted the Red Army right of passage at a desperate point in the Polish defence

The final battles, September–October 1920

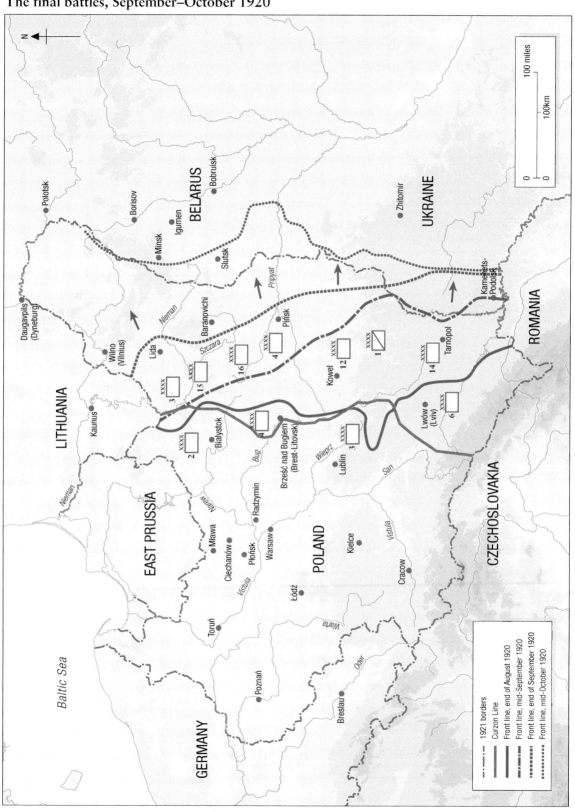

Marshal Józef Piłsudski reviews the troops of the 9th Infantry Division on 4 December 1920 at a ceremony for issuing decorations to the troops for their actions in the Battle of Lida. On the far right of the image is the divisional commander, Brigadier-General Aleksander Narbut-Łuczyński. In front of him is General Edward Śmigły-Rydz, commander of the Strike Group during Piłsudski's August counter-offensive.

effort in July, facilitating the attack of Gai's III Horse Corps into western Poland. Furthermore, Piłsudski and many other senior army commanders had grown up in the region and had no intention of ceding Wilno to Lithuania. To avoid a confrontation with the Entente, Piłsudski suggested to Lucjan Żeligowski, another native of the city, that Polish 'volunteers' should 'rescue' the city from Lithuanian control. In early October, Polish army units began advancing towards Wilno, and an insurrection by Polish residents seized control of the city. Lithuanian army units were unable to resist the Polish advance. On 12 October, Żeligowski declared the formation of 'Central Lithuania'. Piłsudski at this stage hoped to create three Lithuanian 'cantons': the Lithuanian canton with a capital in Kaunus, a Polish canton in Wilno and a Belarussian canton with its capital in Minsk.

In Belarus, Polish troops took Minsk on 15 October. In Ukraine, the Polish army pushed over 100km beyond the Zbruch River, intended to provide Petliura's forces with a foothold in Right-Bank Ukraine beyond likely Polish borders. An armistice took effect on 18 and 19 October. The Polish army was obliged to withdraw back to the tentative borders, including a withdrawal from Minsk. Nevertheless, fighting between Polish allies and the Red Army continued through the end of the year. Petliura's DA-UNR along with allied partisan units continued to fight against the Bolsheviks along the Ukrainian frontier. Likewise, Bułak-Bałachowicz's Belarussian Volunteer Army continued fighting in Belarus. The Treaty of Riga was signed on 18 March 1921, formally ending the war.

AFTERMATH

The Red Army's defeat in the Russo-Polish War of 1919–20 was its only major loss in the Russian Civil Wars of 1917–26. In such an unequal struggle, the Red Army should have won. By the summer of 1920, the Red Army numbered 5 million men, the Polish army not even 1 million. The Red Army had over 70 divisions, the Poles barely 20. Wrangel's threat in Crimea could be easily contained; he hardly managed to mobilize 35,000 troops. There were many reasons for the Red Army's defeat, some of them still controversial.

From a strategic perspective, Lenin's decision to proceed with the conflict at the end of July 1920 snatched defeat from the jaws of victory. By the end of July, the Red Army was approaching the Curzon Line and the Polish army was demoralized and in full retreat. An armistice at this stage would have given Moscow control of the majority of Belarus and Ukraine, albeit at the expense of permitting an independent Polish state. The Entente would have pressured Poland to end the war at this point.

Lenin refused this option based on his strategic intent to Sovietize Poland and provoke a revolution in Western Europe, beginning with Germany. He believed this was achievable due to the momentum of the Red Army's advance in the summer of 1920, his expectation that the Polish working class would revolt and his assumption that the Polish army was on the verge of collapse. This was wishful thinking, distorted by ideological fantasies. A sober assessment would have recalled the volatility of recent campaigns, including the collapse of Deniken's advance in October 1919 and the failure of Piłsudski's Kiev operation in June 1920. Lacking sound logistics, these threadbare armies could easily become exhausted and overextended at the peak of their victory. This made them vulnerable to an equally swift counter-attack, as occurred again in August 1920.

From an operational perspective, the Red Army lacked unity of command. The dual-track military/political command system diffused the decision-making and made the Red Army vulnerable to distractions from its objectives. Shaposhnikov's original Vistula plan envisioned all seven armies in the Polish theatre converging and destroying the Polish army in a climactic battle for Warsaw. Due to Lenin's revolutionary fantasies about sparking revolution in Germany, the Fourth Army went wandering off into western Poland 'to fight the Versailles Treaty' instead of defeating the Polish army. On the South-Western Front, Lenin, through his representative Iosef Stalin, began distracting the field commanders with suggestions about a future campaign against Wrangel in Crimea or future political opportunities in

A Polish cavalry troop passes through Saxon Square in Warsaw in the late summer of 1920 in front of the Cathedral of St Aleksandr Nevskiy. The construction of this cathedral began in 1893 under the direction of the Russian Governor General of Poland, Iosef V. Gourko, who wrote that the imposing new cathedral would symbolize that 'the Russian Church declares to the world that in the western territory along the Vistula, mighty Orthodox rule has taken root'. With its congregation no longer in Warsaw after the war, the cathedral was dismantled by the Poles in the mid-1920s.

Hungary via Lwów. This deflected three more field armies away from the Warsaw campaign. Further undermining Red Army command and control was Kamenev's weak leadership. Intimidated by some of the Bolshevik leaders, he was bullied and ignored by field commanders and their RVSR political overseers.

Red Army decision-making was undermined by poor intelligence. Traditional methods of tactical intelligence gathering were competently done, but there was indifference to new techniques such as air reconnaissance and signals intelligence. In contrast, the Poles believed that intelligence was a vital weapon for the weaker side. Aviation was widely used for deep reconnaissance. Polish exploitation of signals intelligence often was decisive in the decision-making process at the strategic, operational and tactical levels. Piłsudski was an avid fan of signals intelligence, insisting that the cypher bureau telephone him whenever a significant message was decrypted, and often before it was translated. Another intelligence advantage was that many Poles understood Russian, while few Russians understood Polish. The 'Miracle on the Vistula' was heavily dependent on this intelligence advantage, a factor that remained hidden until 2004.

MILITARY LOSSES

The Soviet Union never published comprehensive data on the military casualties of the Russo-Polish War. After the collapse of the Soviet Union, a commission under General Grigoriy F. Krivosheyev attempted to reconstruct Soviet casualty data based on often incomplete data. The table below provides a rough sketch of loss from the 2010 expanded edition of the report. There are obvious problems with the data, for example the unusually low number of wounded in the column of the South-Western Front.

Red Army casualties in the Polish theatre in 1920

	Western Front	South-Western Front	Total
KIA	6,989	10,653	17,642
MIA	53,805	41,075	94,880
Non-combat losses	11,597	5,949	17,546
Sub-total (irrevocable losses)	72,391	57,677	130,068
Wounded	38,861	6,653	45,514
Sick	33,171	23,234	56,405
Total	**144,423**	**87,564**	**231,987**

Source: G. F. Krivosheyev et al., *Rossiya i SSSR v voynakh XX veka: Kniga poteri*, 2010.

Total Polish military casualties between November 1918 and December 1920 were 251,329, of which the combat casualties were 195,207. This included 30,338 killed, 113,518 wounded and 51,351 missing. The majority of these casualties were suffered in the 1920 fighting, with a total of about 157,000 combat casualties in 1920, including about 19,000 killed, 89,000 wounded and 49,000 missing.

There is no comprehensive data of civilian casualties in the Borderlands during these conflicts. Diseases such as typhus and cholera were rampant at this time. Along with famine, non-combat causes probably accounted for the majority of civilian casualties. Intercommunal ethnic violence was also commonplace, and anti-Jewish pogroms added to the grim toll.

Russian museums contain a number of relics from the 1920 war, including this Izhorskiy-Fiat armoured car in Moscow. A total of 81 of these were built by the Izhorskiy Plant near Petrograd in 1917 and 1918 on the basis of Fiat-55 chassis imported from the Fiat Co. of Poughkeepsie, New York. This was the most widely used Russian armoured car of the civil war period next to the various types built on the British Austin chassis.

ECHOES OF THE PAST

The repercussions of the Russo-Polish War have echoed through the past century. Iosef Stalin, a key political ally of Lenin, was reprimanded by the Party over the First Horse Army controversies detailed earlier. After becoming the Soviet dictator in the wake of Lenin's death, Stalin exacted his revenge. The *Holodomor*, the politically inspired famine in Ukraine in 1932 and 1933, can be traced back, at least in part, to Stalin's experiences of the Ukrainian independence movement and the Ukrainian peasant uprisings in Ukraine in 1919 and 1920. The clearest link between the

1920 war and political repression in the USSR was the virtual annihilation of a generation of Red Army commanders, starting with Mikhail Tukhachevskiy in the summer of 1937. Nearly all of the major commanders of the 1920 campaign were executed on Stalin's orders, the main exceptions being Semën Budënniy and the commanders associated with the First Horse Army. These cavalry commanders escaped execution, and led the Red Army in the summer of 1941, the greatest debacle in Soviet military history.

The disputes over the control of the Borderlands did not end in 1921. When the Soviet Union invaded Poland along with its erstwhile ally Nazi Germany in 1939, Moscow took over the contested regions of Belarus and Ukraine. In 1940, the Baltic States and portions of Romania were absorbed back into the empire. In 1945, Stalin succeeded where Lenin had failed in 1920, Sovietizing Central Europe, including Poland. Moscow's control crumbled in 1989, and the Soviet Union itself disintegrated in 1991. An independent Ukraine and Belarus finally emerged out of the Soviet wreckage. Yet even these borders remain contested in view of Moscow's role in the war in eastern Ukraine in 2014.

THE BATTLEFIELDS TODAY

The borders of this battlefield have changed repeatedly over the past century, and many of the same sites were involved in World War II battles. Many memorials to the 1920 battles were erased during the political and military upheavals over the past century. There has been an upsurge of interest in the 1918–20 wars in Poland, Ukraine and the Baltic States, but indifference remains in Russia and Belarus. There are many artefacts associated with the war in museums throughout the region, as shown in some of the accompanying photos.

A machine-gun *tachanka* of the 23rd Tsaritsyn Regiment of the 4th Petrograd Cavalry Division, First Horse Army armed with a 7.62mm Maxim machine gun and preserved at the Central Armed Forces Museum in Moscow.

FURTHER READING

Historical coverage of the 1920 Russo-Polish War is far more extensive in Polish than in Russian. This is not entirely surprising, since the war was central to the emergence of modern Poland, while the Russo-Polish War was only one aspect of the much larger Russian Civil Wars. After Mikhail Tukhachevskiy published a small booklet on the war based on his 7–10 February lectures at the Moscow Military Academy, Piłsudski wrote a lengthy rebuttal that appeared in Polish in 1927 and in English in 1972; the English edition contains the Tukhachevskiy account as well. Polish writing about the war largely ended after the Soviet takeover in 1945. It revived again in the 1990s, including the reprint of many of the classics. Recent Polish scholarship has explored previously secret aspects of the war, such as Nowik's groundbreaking two-volume study of Polish signals intelligence. Appropriately entitled *Before Enigma was Broken*, in reference to later Polish signals-intelligence successes against the German Enigma cyphers, this massive study examines not only the codebreaking, but also provides details on the type of data uncovered by the decypherment efforts.

Russian accounts of the war flourished in the early 1920s. Tukhachevskiy's 1923 report provoked a spirited debate about the Battle of Warsaw in subsequent histories, including Shaposhnikov's short account. Kakurin's Red Army staff study remains the most detailed account from the Russian perspective. With Stalin's rise to power, it became increasingly dangerous to write about the Russo-Polish War except for hagiographies of Budënniy and the exploits of the First Horse Army. In spite of the de-Stalinization of the Khrushchev years, there have been few detailed studies of the campaign published in recent years.

Most of the Ukrainian accounts of the campaign were published in exile over the years, especially in Poland and Canada. Since the collapse of the Soviet Union, there has been renewed interest in this subject in Ukraine, with some specialized studies beginning to appear.

There are a number of excellent campaign accounts in English by Davies and Zamoyski. An increasing number of specialized academic studies have appeared over the past few decades, heavily oriented on the diplomatic and political aspects of the conflict.

Böhler, Jochen, *Civil War in Central Europe 1918–1921: The Reconstruction of Poland*, Oxford University Press, Oxford: 2019

Brown, Stephen, *The First Cavalry Army in the Russian Civil War 1918–1920*, PhD dissertation, University of Wollongong: 1990

Danilov, Ivan, *Podzabytaya voyna: Polsko-sovetskaya voyna 1920 goda i ee posledstviya*, Smeltok, Minsk: 2016

Davies, Norman, *White Eagle, Red Star: The Polish Soviet War 1919–20*, Macdonald, London: 1972

Gritskevich, A. P., *Zapadniy front RSFSR 1918–1920: Borba mezhdu Rossiey i Polsey za Belorussiyu*, Kharvest, Minsk: 2008

Kakurin, N. E. and Melikov, V. A., *Voyna s belopolyakami 1920 goda*, Voenizdat, Moscow: 1925

Khromov, S.S., *Grazhdanskaya voyna i voennaya interventsiya v SSSR*, Sovetskaya Entsiklopediya, Moscow: 1983

Knyt, Agnieszka et al., *The Year 1920: The War between Poland and Bolshevik Russia*, Warsaw History Museum, Warsaw: 2005

Kondratiuk, Leonid, *Ukrainian Galician Army in the Ukrainian-Polish War 1918–1919*, master's thesis, Kansas State University: 1979

Kutrzeba, Tadeusz, *Wyprawa Kijówska 1920 roku*, Druk Narodowa, Kraków: 1937

Lipinski, Wacław, *Walka zbrojna o niepodległość polski 1905–1918*, Instytut Badania Najnowszej Historji Polski, Warsaw: 1935

Łukomski, Grzegorz, *Walka rzeczypospolitej o kresy północno-wschodnie 1918–1920*, Mickiewicz University Press, Poznań: 1994

—— and Polak, Bogusław, *W obronie Wilna, Grodna i Mińska: Front Litewsko-Białoruski wojny polsko-bolszewickiej 1918–1920*, Wyższej Szkoly Inżynierskiej, Koszalin: 1994

Lundgreen-Nielsen, Kay, *The Polish Problem at the Paris Peace Conference 1918–1919*, Odense University Press, Odense: 1979

Marievskiy, I. P., *Sovetsko-polskaya voyna 1920 goda*, Frunze Academy, Moscow: 1941

Musialik, Zdzisław, *General Weygand and the Battle of the Vistula 1920*, Piłsudski Institute, London: 1987

Nevezhin, K., *Russko-polskaya voyna 1919–1920 goda*, Voenakadem, Moscow: 1923

Nowak, Włodzimierz, *Komarów 1920*, Bellona, Warsaw: 2014

Nowik, Grzegorz, *Zanim złamano 'Enigmę': Polski radiowywiad podczas wojny z bolszewicką Rosją 1918–1920*, Wyd. Rytm, Warsaw: Vol. 1: 2004, Vol. 2: 2010

Odziemkowski, Janusz, *Leksykon wojny polsko-rosyjskiej 1919–1920*, Rytm, Warsaw: 2004

—— and Rukkas, Andrij, *Polska-Ukraina 1920*, Wyd. Volumen, Warsaw: 2017

Palij, Michael, *The Ukrainian–Polish Defensive Alliance 1919–1921*, Canadian Institute of Ukrainian Studies, Toronto: 1995

Piłsudski, Józef, *Year 1920 and its Climax: The Battle of Warsaw during the Polish-Soviet War 1919–1920*, Piłsudski Institute, New York: 1972

Pipes, Richard, *The Unknown Lenin: From the Secret Archives*, Yale University Press, New Haven: 1998

Shaposnikov, Boris, *Na Visle: K istorii kampanii 1920 goda*, Voenizdat, Moscow: 1924

Sikorski, Władysław, *Nad Wisłą i Wkrą: Studium z polsko-rosyjskiej wojny 1920 roku*, Lwów: 1928/reprint Wyd. 2 Kolory: Warsaw: 2017

Stachiewicz, Juljan, *Studia operacyjne z historji wojen polskich 1918–21, Tom I: Działania zaczepne 3 armji na Ukrainie*, General Staff Historical Office, Warsaw: 1925

Stryjek, Jarosław, *Warszawa 1920: Walki o Radzymin, Wołomin i Ossów*, Taktyka i Strategia, Warsaw: 2011

Tarkowski, Krzystof, *Lotnictwo polskie w wojnie z rosją sowiecką 1919–1920*, WKL, Warsaw: 1991

Vitkus, Gediminas (ed.), *Wars of Lithuania: A Systematic Quantitative Analysis of Lithuania's Wars in the 19th and 20th Centuries*, General Jonas Žemaitas Academy, Vilnius: 2014

Waligóra, Bolesław, *Bitwa Warszawska 1920: Bój pod Ossowem i Leśniakowizną w dniu 14 VIII 1920 r.*, Wojskowe Biuro Historyczne, Warsaw: 1932

Wyszczelski, Lech, *Warszawa 1920*, Bellona, Warsaw: 1995

Zamoyski, Adam, *The Battle for the Marchlands*, Columbia University Press: New York: 1981

——, *Warsaw 1920: Lenin's Failed Conquest of Europe*, Harper Collins, London: 2008

INDEX